New England Bed & Breakfast Cookbook

New England Bed & Breakfast Cookbook

Copyright © 2004 3D Press, Inc. All rights reserved.

No part of this book may be used or reproduced in any manner whatsoever or stored in a database or retrieval system, without prior written permission from the publisher, except for the inclusion of brief quotations in a review.

First Edition

ISBN 1-889593-12-5

Printed in China

Design: Lisa Bachar & Tracey Ranta
Editing: Carol Faino & Susan Larson

Cover Photos: Robert Harding World Imagery (top)
Ellen Silverman (bottom)

3D Press, Inc.
655 Broadway, Suite 560
Denver, Colorado 80203
303-623-4484 (phone)
303-623-4494 (fax)
info@3dpress.net

888-456-3607 (order toll-free)
www.3dpress.net

The Bed & Breakfast Cookbook Series™ was originated by Carol Faino & Doreen Hazledine of Peppermint Press in Denver, Colorado in 1996.

Disclaimer and Limits of Liability
Recipes and descriptions of the inns featured in this book are based on information supplied to the publisher, 3D Press, Inc., from sources believed to be reliable. While the publisher has used its best efforts to insure the accuracy of all information at press time, the passage of time will always bring about change. Therefore, the publisher does not guarantee the accuracy or completeness of any information and is not responsible for any errors or omissions, or the results obtained from use of such information. The reader assumes sole responsibility for any injury or illness associated with preparation of the recipes. The recipes chosen for inclusion in this book are claimed to be original or adapted as noted. Recipes are reprinted as provided to the publisher, though the publisher did edit recipes for clarity. This book is sold as is, without warranty of any kind, either expressed or implied. Neither the authors nor 3D Press, Inc. nor its distributors shall be liable to the purchaser or any other person or entity with respect to any liability, loss, or damage caused or alleged to be caused directly or indirectly by this book.

Introduction

The *New England Bed & Breakfast Cookbook* is a culinary doorway to New England's charms. With sandy beaches, breathtaking mountains, lush forests and cities steeped in culture and history, New England is one of the most spectacular areas of the country. The *New England Bed & Breakfast Cookbook* brings a taste of each state in the region, with recipes from family-run bed & breakfasts and luxury inns alike in Connecticut, Maine, Massachusetts, New Hampshire, Rhode Island and Vermont.

Recipes are as diverse as the inns and the landscape, and each provides a unique taste of New England. Some recipes are family heirlooms. Others make use of the local dairy products, maple syrup, seafood and produce for which New England is famous. All of the inns share something in common – their gracious hospitality and love of New England.

Visit the Mountains … In winter, New England boasts world-class skiing. Enjoy fluffy homemade waffles sweetened with real Vermont Maple syrup before sliding down the slopes at Killington in Vermont or Sugarloaf in Maine. In summer, hike and bike on exquisite, wildflower-specked trails.

Visit the Countryside … There is no better place to relax than a swaying hammock overlooking Vermont's rolling hillsides. Explore the skyscraping granite crests of New Hampshire's White Mountains. In autumn, New England's fiery sugar maples, punctuated by the white steeples of historic churches, are some of the most breathtaking sights in the world.

Visit the Coast … From the beaches of Cape Cod to the rocky coast of Maine, New England offers a great variety of coastal byways. Gather sand dollars on the Connecticut shore, take a whale watching cruise in Nantucket, view Maine's lobster boats depart in the morning or stroll along the beach.

Revisit the Past … Walk along Boston's historic Freedom trail and visit the church whose lanterns guided Paul Revere. Visit Newport, where exquisite historic mansions tower above spectacular rocky cliffs. Visit Portland, Maine, an important shipping center during the American Revolution.

Whether you are a New England resident or a visitor who loves the area's grace and charm, the *New England Bed & Breakfast Cookbook* is an ideal way to preserve and recreate the magic of this special region time and again.

We hope you enjoy it as much as we do!

Melissa Craven & Jordan Salcito

About the Authors

Melissa Craven was the oldest child in a career Air Force family. She has lived in seven states, granting her an appreciation for the diverse flavors and food cultures of the United States. As an adult, she is not afraid to try new things in the kitchen. With experience in journalism, recipe testing, marketing and public relations she understands the need for clear and concise recipes. As a cook, she understands the joy that comes from creating memorable meals for family and friends. She melds her knowledge and interests to create consistently winning recipes. Melissa is also the author of the *Colorado Farmers' Market Cookbook*, *Virginia Bed & Breakfast Cookbook* and co-author of *Red White & Blue Ribbon 2004*. She will co-author the soon-to-be-released *California Bed & Breakfast Cookbook* and is also a contributing editor in the other Bed & Breakfast Cookbook Series.

Jordan Salcito, a Colorado native, moved to the East Coast for college where she majored in English Literature. Having spent time with family in Vermont and Massachusetts, and having lived in both Pennsylvania and New York, she has garnered a love for the charm and beauty of New England. With a background in writing and literature and a lifelong passion for cuisine, she has been able to merge her two loves in the *New England Bed & Breakfast Cookbook*. Jordan has worked in restaurants as a bartender, host, server, manager and sous chef, and understands the love and joy that comes from creating a meal for others. This is Jordan's second cookbook – she is also co-author of *Red White & Blue Ribbon 2004*. She has also written restaurant reviews for The Denver Post and will co-author the soon-to-be-released *California Bed & Breakfast Cookbook*.

Table of Contents

Breads & Muffins 6

Coffee Cakes, Scones, Granola & Oatmeal 46

Pancakes & Waffles 68

French Toast, Bread Pudding & Crêpes.............................96

Egg Dishes & Breakfast Entrées 126

Side Dishes, Soups & Salads 160

Appetizers 192

Luncheon & Dinner Entrées 212

Fruit Specialties 234

Desserts 262

Geographic Listing of Bed & Breakfasts 304

Alphabetical Listing of Bed & Breakfasts.......................308

Index of Recipes..312

Breads & Muffins

Lemon Poppy Seed Bread 9

Bobby's Blueberry Bread 11

Cranberry-Orange Christmas Bread 13

Banana Bread with Streusel Topping..15

Blueberry Gingerbread 17

Pull-Apart Bread 19

Blue & Yellow Cornmeal Layered Pound Cake..............................21

Goat Cheese Popovers..23

Westbrook Inn Spinach Bread 25

Vermont Cheddar Wafers 27

Maple Walnut Muffins 29

Banana Oatmeal Almond Muffins 31

Pumpkin Chocolate Chip Muffins 33

Cappuccino Chocolate Chip Muffins 35

Sweet Potato Muffins or Bread 37

Flat-Top Orange Date Muffins 39

Apple Muffins..41

Blueberry Cream Muffins 43

Apple or Carrot Bran Muffins...45

Breads & Muffins

The Bow Street Inn

The Bow Street Inn is housed in a historic, 19th century brick brewery storage building, renovated in the 1980s, with the Bow Street Inn opening on the upper floor and the Seacoast Repertory Theatre taking over the first floor. The inn is within easy walking distance of all the restaurants, theaters, shops, historic homes and museums that Portsmouth has to offer.

The inn consists of ten rooms decorated in a country Victorian style, with queen-size brass beds and private baths. Two of the rooms offer views of Portsmouth's working harbor.

INNKEEPERS:	Joan & Art Jones
ADDRESS:	121 Bow Street
	Portsmouth, New Hampshire 03801
TELEPHONE:	(603) 431-7760
E-MAIL:	bowstreetinn@aol.com
WEBSITE:	www.bowstreetinn.com
ROOMS:	10 Rooms; Private baths
CHILDREN:	Children age 5 and older welcome
ANIMALS:	Not allowed
HANDICAPPED:	Not handicapped accessible
DIETARY NEEDS:	Will accommodate guests' special dietary needs

Lemon Poppy Seed Bread

Makes 1 Loaf

"As part of our expanded continental breakfast, we serve many kinds of breads. This is a favorite of our guests – the addition of poppy seeds makes it a hit!" - Innkeeper, The Bow Street Inn

- 1 tablespoon plus ⅓ cup lemonade concentrate
- 1 stick butter, softened
- 2 large eggs
- 1 cup sugar
- 1½ cups all-purpose flour
- ¼ teaspoon salt
- 1 teaspoon baking powder
- ½ cup milk
- 2 tablespoons plus 1 teaspoon poppy seeds

Preheat oven to 350°F. Combine 1 tablespoon of lemonade concentrate, butter, eggs, sugar, flour, salt, baking powder milk and 2 tablespoons of poppy seeds. Beat with a mixer on medium speed for 3 minutes. Pour batter into a greased 9x5-inch loaf pan. Bake for 55-60 minutes, or until a toothpick inserted in center comes out clean.

Remove bread from oven. Spread ⅓ cup of lemonade concentrate over top of hot bread. Sprinkle bread with 1 teaspoon of poppy seeds. Serve warm or at room temperature.

Inn at Crystal Lake

Keeping watch over the charming lakeside village of Eaton, the award-winning Inn at Crystal Lake is a touchstone for service and hospitality in the Mt. Washington Valley. Located at the historic 1884 Palmer House, just minutes from North Conway, this charming New England inn provides a traditional bed & breakfast atmosphere with the refinement of a small European hotel.

"You have created the model for the perfect New England inn. Attentive care, excellent food and charming ambiance." ~ Guests, Lehigh Valley, PA

INNKEEPERS:	Bobby Barker & Tim Ostendorf
ADDRESS:	Route 153
	Eaton Center, New Hampshire 03832
TELEPHONE:	(603) 447-2120; (800) 343-7336
E-MAIL:	stay@innatcrystallake.com
WEBSITE:	www.innatcrystallake.com
ROOMS:	11 Rooms; 1 Cottage; Private baths
CHILDREN:	Children age 10 and older welcome
ANIMALS:	Dogs welcome (1 room); Resident cats
HANDICAPPED:	Not handicapped accessible
DIETARY NEEDS:	Will accommodate guests' special dietary needs

Bobby's Blueberry Bread

Makes 8 Servings

"This recipe was chosen by Yankee Magazine for their 2002 Bed & Breakfast Guide." ~ Innkeeper, Inn at Crystal Lake

1	stick butter, softened
1½	cups sugar, plus extra for topping
1	cup sour cream
3	eggs
3	cups all-purpose flour, sifted
4	teaspoons baking powder
1	teaspoon salt
2	cups fresh blueberries

Preheat oven to 350°F. Combine butter, sugar and sour cream. Add eggs and mix well. Add flour, baking powder and salt and mix just until batter comes together. Fold in blueberries.

Pour batter into a greased and floured tube or Bundt pan. Sprinkle a layer of sugar over batter. Bake for 1 hour (check after 45 minutes), until a toothpick inserted in center comes out clean.

Tip: In fall, substitute fresh cranberries and walnuts for the blueberries.

The Gables Inn

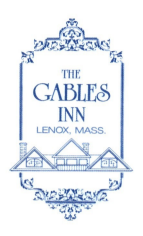

The Gables Inn is a fully recreated, 100-year-old classic Berkshire 'cottage' built in the Queen Anne style and fully capturing the true essence and elegant style of the late 19th century. To visit the inn is to travel back in time. The innkeepers have lovingly adorned the inn with authentic period furnishings and graced it with rare documents and books and a collection of fine art that spans five centuries.

Only a mile from Tanglewood in the heart of historic Lenox, the inn offers lavishly decorated rooms, heated indoor swimming pool and tennis court.

INNKEEPERS:	Mary & Frank Newton
ADDRESS:	81 Walker Street (Route 183)
	Lenox, Massachusetts 01240
TELEPHONE:	(413) 637-3416; (800) 382-9401
E-MAIL:	gables@berkshire.net
WEBSITE:	www.gableslenox.com
ROOMS:	13 Rooms; 4 Suites; Private baths
CHILDREN:	Children age 12 and older welcome
ANIMALS:	Not allowed
HANDICAPPED:	Not handicapped accessible
DIETARY NEEDS:	Cannot accommodate guests' special dietary needs

Cranberry-Orange Christmas Bread

Makes 1 Loaf

2	tablespoons vegetable oil
1	large egg
1	cup orange juice
1	cup sugar
2	cups all-purpose flour
½	teaspoon salt
1½	teaspoons baking powder
½	teaspoon baking soda
1	cup fresh or frozen cranberries

Preheat oven to 350°F. In a large bowl, combine oil, egg, orange juice and sugar. In a medium bowl, combine flour, salt, baking powder and baking soda; add to egg mixture and stir just until flour mixture is moistened. Stir in cranberries. Bake in a greased 9x5-inch loaf pan for 60 minutes, or until a toothpick inserted in center comes out clean.

The Morrison House

The Morrison House Bed & Breakfast, a charming, Italianate, turn-of-the-century house, is a tranquil home-away-from-home in the heart of one of America's most vibrant neighborhoods. Just a few minutes walk from the Davis Square subway station, the inn is conveniently located near Tufts, Harvard and downtown Boston. The Minuteman Bikeway, which runs through Arlington and Lexington into Bedford, is a block away.

A continental-plus breakfast is served in the sunny, airy dining room or, weather permitting, on the secluded patio.

INNKEEPERS:	Ron & Linde Dynneson
ADDRESS:	221 Morrison Avenue
	Somerville, Massachusetts 02144
TELEPHONE:	(617) 627-9670; (877) 627-9670
E-MAIL:	hosts@morrisonhousebnb.com
WEBSITE:	www.morrisonhousebnb.com
ROOMS:	12 Rooms; Private baths
CHILDREN:	Welcome
ANIMALS:	Not allowed; Resident cat
HANDICAPPED:	Not handicapped accessible
DIETARY NEEDS:	Will accommodate guests' special dietary needs

Banana Bread with Streusel Topping

Makes 1 Loaf

"One day, I was making banana bread and topped it with some leftover streusel topping. It was such a big hit that I've been making it this way every since." ~ Innkeeper, The Morrison House Bed & Breakfast

Banana bread:
1¾	cups all-purpose flour
½	teaspoon salt
1¼	teaspoons cream of tartar
¾	teaspoon baking soda
5⅓	tablespoons butter, softened
⅔	cup sugar
1	teaspoon vanilla extract
2	large eggs, well beaten
3	very ripe, large bananas, mashed
½	cup coarsely chopped walnuts

Streusel topping:
½	cup packed brown sugar
½	cup chopped walnuts
2	tablespoons butter, melted
½	teaspoon cinnamon
2	tablespoons all-purpose flour

Preheat oven to 350°F. In a large bowl, cream together butter, sugar and vanilla. Mix in eggs, 1 at a time. Add bananas, mix well. In a medium bowl, whisk together flour, salt, cream of tartar and baking soda; add to butter mixture and mix just until moistened. Stir in nuts. Pour batter into a greased 9x5-inch loaf pan. Sprinkle streusel topping over batter. Bake for 50-60 minutes, or until a toothpick inserted in center comes out clean.

For the streusel topping: Combine all streusel ingredients until crumbly.

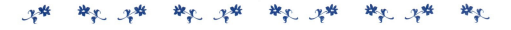

The Inn at Southwest

The Inn at Southwest is a circa 1884 Victorian bed & breakfast that overlooks the serene waters of Southwest Harbor. Near the center of town and close to Bar Harbor and Acadia National Park, the inn offers comfortable yet elegant lodging and is within walking distance of shops, restaurants and the marina.

Rooms have down-filled duvets, ceiling fans and luxurious linens and towels. Some rooms feature limited water views and gas log stoves. Freshly baked cookies and refreshments welcome you back from a day's activities.

INNKEEPERS:	Andrea Potapovs & Sandy Johnson
ADDRESS:	371 Main Street
	Southwest Harbor, Maine 04679
TELEPHONE:	(207) 244-3835
E-MAIL:	reservations@innatsouthwest.com
WEBSITE:	www.innatsouthwest.com
ROOMS:	5 Rooms; 2 Suites; Private baths
CHILDREN:	Children age 8 and older welcome
ANIMALS:	Not allowed
HANDICAPPED:	Not handicapped accessible
DIETARY NEEDS:	Will accommodate guests' special dietary needs

Blueberry Gingerbread

Makes 9 Servings

½	cup vegetable oil
1	cup plus 2 tablespoons sugar
1	egg
½	cup molasses
1	cup fresh or frozen blueberries
2	cups all-purpose flour
1	teaspoon baking soda
1	teaspoon cinnamon
½	teaspoon ground ginger
½	teaspoon nutmeg
½	teaspoon salt
1	cup buttermilk

Preheat oven to 350°F. In a large bowl, beat oil, sugar and egg with a mixer on medium speed until light. Add molasses and beat at high speed for 2 minutes. In a medium bowl, combine flour, baking soda, cinnamon, ginger, nutmeg and salt; add to molasses mixture alternately with buttermilk and beat until smooth. Fold in blueberries. Pour batter into a greased 9x9-inch baking pan. Bake for about 60 minutes, or until middle is set and a toothpick inserted in center comes out clean. Cool slightly before serving.

Homespun Farm

Homespun literally means "handmade," which perfectly describes this Colonial farmhouse listed on the National Register of Historic Places. The house has been tenderly transformed into a warm, romantic, relaxing, bed & breakfast located near Mystic Seaport, New London submarine base, hiking, the University of Connecticut and many other attractions.

Rooms feature a fireplace, bathrobes and many other luxurious amenities. Surround yourself in a sea of fine linens and pillows, then wake to a full country breakfast served by candlelight.

INNKEEPERS:	Kate & Ron Bauer
ADDRESS:	306 Preston Road, Route 164
	Griswold, Connecticut 06351
TELEPHONE:	(860) 376-5178; (888) 889-6673
E-MAIL:	relax@homespunfarm.com
WEBSITE:	www.homespunfarm.com
ROOMS:	3 Rooms; 1 Suite; Private baths
CHILDREN:	Welcome
ANIMALS:	Welcome; call ahead
HANDICAPPED:	Not handicapped accessible
DIETARY NEEDS:	Will accommodate guests' special dietary needs

Pull-Apart Bread

Makes 4 to 6 Servings

Plan ahead – this bread needs to be started the night before.

- 1   (12-ounce) package frozen yeast dinner rolls
- 1   (3½-ounce) package butterscotch pudding
- 1   cup brown sugar
- 2   tablespoons cinnamon
- 1   stick butter, melted
- ½   chopped cup pecans (optional)

Put frozen rolls in a greased tube cake pan. Sprinkle with pudding, brown sugar and cinnamon. Drizzle melted butter over ingredients in pan. Sprinkle with pecans, if desired. Cover and let stand in an unheated oven overnight.

The next day, preheat oven to 350°F. Bake bread for about 30 minutes, until done. Remove from oven and immediately turn out onto a serving plate. Serve warm or at room temperature.

Rabbit Hill Inn

Established in 1795, the Rabbit Hill Inn is an elegant, luxury country inn – a perfect Vermont destination for relaxing escapes, romantic getaways and honeymoons. Select from 19 romantic, lavishly appointed guest rooms and suites – most with glowing fireplaces, many with double whirlpool tubs, canopy beds and antiques. All rooms are steeped with charm and elegance, designed with your needs and comforts in mind.

"There are some inns that just seem to stir the romantic soul and this show piece is most certainly one of them!" ~ The Travel Channel

INNKEEPERS:	Brian & Leslie Mulcahy
ADDRESS:	48 Lower Waterford Road
	Lower Waterford, Vermont 05848
TELEPHONE:	(802) 748-5168; (800) 762-8669
E-MAIL:	info@rabbithillinn.com
WEBSITE:	www.rabbithillinn.com
ROOMS:	11 Rooms; 8 Suites; Private baths
CHILDREN:	Children age 13 and older welcome
ANIMALS:	Not allowed
HANDICAPPED:	Handicapped accessible
DIETARY NEEDS:	Will accommodate guests' special dietary needs

Blue & Yellow Cornmeal Layered Pound Cake

Makes 8 to 10 Servings

This beautiful, unique poundcake has two layers, one of blue cornmeal and one of yellow cornmeal. Serve with Lobster Gazpacho (see recipe on page 179).

2	sticks butter, softened and divided
1	cup sugar, divided
6	eggs, divided
2	cups corn, divided
½	cup sour cream, divided
1½	cups all-purpose flour, divided
½	teaspoon salt, divided
¼	cup blue cornmeal
¼	cup yellow cornmeal

Preheat oven to 350°F. In a bowl, cream together 1 stick of butter and ½ cup of sugar. Mix in 3 eggs and 1 cup of corn. Stir in ¼ cup of sour cream, ¾ cup of flour, ¼ teaspoon of salt and blue cornmeal; set aside.

In a separate bowl, cream together 1 stick of butter and ½ cup of sugar. Mix in 3 eggs and 1 cup of corn. Stir in ¼ cup of sour cream, ¾ cup of flour, ¼ teaspoon of salt and yellow cornmeal.

Spread blue cornmeal mixture in bottom of a greased and floured 9-inch round cake pan. Carefully spread yellow cornmeal mixture over blue cornmeal mixture. Bake for about 30 minutes, until a toothpick inserted in center comes out clean.

White Rocks Inn

Whether the landscape is ablaze with fall color, wrapped in a blanket of snow or bursting with wildflowers and freshly cut hay, you will be sure to create memories of a lifetime at the White Rocks Inn. Each room is a private retreat, lovingly decorated with family heirlooms and antiques to reflect the genteel lifestyle of the mid-1800s.

Set away from the main house, the Milkhouse Cottage is the inn's most private accommodation and is a favorite of honeymooners. It has a loft bed, a fireplace and a deck overlooking the meadow and adjoining farm.

INNKEEPERS:	Malcolm & Rita Swogger
ADDRESS:	1774 U.S. 7 South
	Wallingford, Vermont 05773
TELEPHONE:	(802) 446-2077; (866) 446-2077
E-MAIL:	info@whiterocksinn.com
WEBSITE:	www.whiterocksinn.com
ROOMS:	5 Rooms; 1 Cottage; Private baths
CHILDREN:	Children welcome; Call ahead
ANIMALS:	Welcome in cottage; Resident dog
HANDICAPPED:	Not handicapped accessible
DIETARY NEEDS:	Will accommodate guests' special dietary needs

Goat Cheese Popovers

Makes 24 Popovers

Vegetable oil
6 eggs
1½ cups all-purpose flour
1 teaspoon salt
½ teaspoon pepper
Pinch of nutmeg
2 cups milk
½ cup heavy cream
4 ounces herbed goat cheese, chilled and cut into 24 pieces

Preheat oven to 400°F. Brush muffin cups with oil and heat oven. Blend eggs, flour, salt, pepper and nutmeg in a blender for about 10 seconds, until well combined. Scrape down sides. With blender running, slowly pour in milk and cream; blend until smooth.

Remove muffin tins from oven. Fill each muffin cup ½-full with batter. Place a piece of goat cheese in center of batter in each muffin cup. Top with enough batter to fill cups ⅔-full. Bake for about 40-50 minutes, until puffed and golden. Serve hot.

Westbrook Inn

Westbrook Inn Bed & Breakfast was built in 1876 by a local sea captain. Extra rooms were used to house travelers and seamen who passed through Westbrook. Over the years, it became part of an annex for a famous resort that housed actors vacationing from New York. Today, this beautifully restored, four-season inn has ten charming rooms plus a two-bedroom cottage complete with a full kitchen.

In addition to lovely accommodations, guests are treated to the inn's famous three-course breakfast each morning.

INNKEEPERS:	Glenn & Chris Monroe
ADDRESS:	976 Boston Post Road
	Westbrook, Connecticut 06498
TELEPHONE:	(860) 399-4777; (800) 342-3162
E-MAIL:	info@westbrookinn.com
WEBSITE:	www.westbrookinn.com
ROOMS:	10 Rooms; 1 Cottage; Private baths
CHILDREN:	Children welcome
ANIMALS:	Not allowed
HANDICAPPED:	Handicapped accessible
DIETARY NEEDS:	Will accommodate guests' special dietary needs

Westbrook Inn Spinach Bread

Makes 12 Servings

"Probably good reheated the next day – too bad there's never any left!" - Innkeeper, Westbrook Inn Bed & Breakfast

¼	cup olive oil
1	tablespoon butter
½	green or red bell pepper, diced small
1	medium onion, chopped
½	(7-ounce) can sliced mushrooms or 6 ounces fresh mushrooms, sliced
1	clove garlic, chopped
1	(10-ounce) package frozen spinach, thawed in microwave

Pinch of cayenne pepper
Freshly ground pepper, to taste
Pinch of parsley
Pinch of basil
Pinch of oregano
1 teaspoon garlic powder
Pinch of crushed red pepper
Pinch of salt
1 pound pizza dough or bread dough
4 slices provolone cheese
1½ cups grated mozzarella cheese
2 tablespoons Romano cheese
Cornmeal

Preheat oven to 350°F. Heat olive oil and butter in a skillet over medium heat. Add bell peppers and onions; cook until soft. Add mushrooms and chopped garlic; cook until mushrooms are soft. Add spinach and spices; cook for 1-2 minutes. Add more olive oil if mixture looks too dry.

Roll dough into a thin oval shape. Spread bell pepper mixture over dough. Top with cheeses. Roll up jelly-roll style; seal ends and seams well. Place on a baking sheet brushed with a light coat of oil and sprinkled with cornmeal. Bake for 30 minutes, or until lightly browned on top.

Hartwell House Inn

The Hartwell House Inn offers elegant accommodations with authentic New England charm. Rooms are furnished with a distinctive collection of early American and English antiques. Most have French doors leading to terraces or balconies overlooking sculpted flower gardens.

The inn's expansive landscape, with its picturesque lily pond and manicured croquet lawn, offers the beauty and tranquility of the Maine countryside. Yet, the inn is ideally located within walking distance of all that Ogunquit has to offer. A full, gourmet breakfast and afternoon tea are served each day.

INNKEEPERS:	Paul & Gail Koehler
ADDRESS:	312 Shore Road
	Ogunquit, Maine 03907
TELEPHONE:	(207) 646-7210; (800) 235-8883
E-MAIL:	info@hartwellhouseinn.com
WEBSITE:	www.hartwellhouseinn.com
ROOMS:	13 Rooms; 3 Suites; Private baths
CHILDREN:	Children age 16 and older welcome
ANIMALS:	Not allowed
HANDICAPPED:	Not handicapped accessible
DIETARY NEEDS:	Will accommodate guests' special dietary needs

Vermont Cheddar Wafers

Makes 18 Wafers

"With just a hint of spice, these wafers are the perfect snack any time of day." ~ Innkeeper, Hartwell House Inn

1	pound Vermont sharp cheddar cheese, grated
2	sticks butter, softened
2¼	cups all-purpose flour
½	teaspoon salt
½	teaspoon white pepper
¼	teaspoon cayenne pepper

Preheat oven to 350°F. Combine all ingredients with a stand mixer using the dough hook attachment (or use a wooden spoon). Roll dough into 1-inch-thick round logs. Chill dough for at least 30 minutes. Slice dough into ⅛-inch-thick slices. Bake on a cookie sheet for about 12 minutes, until golden brown.

Sugar Hill Inn

The Sugar Hill Inn is a historic farmhouse built in 1789 and impeccably restored over the years to its present beauty. Throughout the year, the inn offers packages for getaways, the holidays and special events. The Maple Sugaring Weekend includes a two-hour program depicting the history and production of maple sugar, a horse-drawn wagon ride and a five-course dinner featuring maple syrup in each course – from soup to dessert.

A full breakfast is served and includes such favorites as old-fashioned red flannel hash, gingerbread pancakes and cinnamon-raisin bread French toast.

INNKEEPERS:	Judy & Orlo Coots
ADDRESS:	Scenic Route 117
	Sugar Hill, New Hampshire 03585
TELEPHONE:	(603) 823-5621; (800) 548-4748
E-MAIL:	info@sugarhillinn.com
WEBSITE:	www.sugarhillinn.com
ROOMS:	9 Rooms; 6 Cottages; Private baths
CHILDREN:	Welcome
ANIMALS:	Not allowed
HANDICAPPED:	Not handicapped accessible
DIETARY NEEDS:	Will accommodate guests' special dietary needs

Maple Walnut Muffins

Makes 12 Muffins

"I adapted this from our blueberry muffin recipe to serve during our Maple Sugaring Weekend. They are now the most popular muffin we serve." - Innkeeper, Sugar Hill Inn

1½	cups all-purpose flour
½	teaspoon salt
1	teaspoon baking powder
½	teaspoon baking soda
¼	cup packed brown sugar
1	cup old-fashioned or quick-cooking rolled oats
1	cup sour cream
5	tablespoons butter, softened
2	eggs
¾	cup real maple syrup
1	cup chopped walnuts

Preheat oven to 375°F. Spray medium-size muffin cups with non-stick cooking spray or line with papers liners. In a large bowl, combine flour, salt, baking powder, baking soda, brown sugar and oats. In a medium bowl, combine sour cream, butter, eggs and maple syrup; add to flour mixture and stir to combine. Stir in nuts.

Pour batter into muffin cups. Bake for 20-30 minutes, rotating pan halfway through baking time, until a toothpick inserted in center comes out clean. Let stand for 10 minutes before removing muffins from cups.

The Inn On Cove Hill

Rockport is noted for its stately homes, dramatic coastline and white picket fences festooned with pastel beach roses. Behind one such fence, the Inn on Cove Hill awaits guests in search of old New England-style elegance and beautifully restored Federal- and Georgian-style architecture.

A magnificent entryway, featuring a gracefully handcrafted spiral staircase, greets visitors upon arrival. Beautiful, wide pumpkin pine floorboards, crown and dentil molding and a wood-paneled hallway lead to rooms of exceptional character.

INNKEEPERS:	Betsy F. Eck
ADDRESS:	37 Mount Pleasant Street
	Rockport, Massachusetts 01966
TELEPHONE:	(978) 546-2701; (888) 546-2701
E-MAIL:	beck@ziplink.net
WEBSITE:	www.innoncovehill.com
ROOMS:	8 Rooms; Private & shared baths
CHILDREN:	Children age 12 and older welcome
ANIMALS:	Not allowed
HANDICAPPED:	Not handicapped accessible
DIETARY NEEDS:	Will accommodate guests' special dietary needs

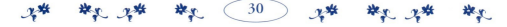

Banana Oatmeal Almond Muffins

Makes 12 Jumbo or 24 Regular Muffins

"I started with a recipe from the former owner of the inn and made it my own." ~ Innkeeper, The Inn On Cove Hill

4-5	well-ripened bananas, mashed
4	large eggs
¼	cup plus 2 tablespoons vanilla yogurt
2	teaspoons vanilla extract
1¾	sticks butter, melted
4	cups all-purpose flour
¾	cup sugar
4	teaspoons baking powder
2	teaspoons baking soda
¾	cup Irish oats
¾	cup sliced almonds

Preheat oven to 375°F. In a large bowl, combine bananas, eggs, yogurt and vanilla. Stir in melted butter. In a medium bowl, combine flour, sugar, baking powder, baking soda, oatmeal and almonds; add to banana mixture and stir until combined.

Pour batter into greased or paper-lined jumbo or regular muffin cups. Bake for 25-30 minutes, or until a toothpick inserted in center comes out clean.

Carriage House of Woodstock

The Carriage House is located in Woodstock, with its year-round recreation, cultural events, antiquing, gallery shopping and other activities. Enjoy nearby cross-country skiing, snowshoeing, ice skating and horse-drawn sleigh rides. Nearby Sugarbush Farms is the perfect place to sample Vermont finest maple syrup, cheeses and other goodies.

Rooms are named after Vermont covered bridges. Many offer fireplaces and gorgeous views of the surrounding area. The inn was named "2003 Top Bed & Breakfast for Viewing Fall Foliage" by *Inn Traveler* magazine.

INNKEEPERS:	Debbie & Mark Stanglin
ADDRESS:	455 Woodstock Road, Route 4 West
	Woodstock, Vermont 05091
TELEPHONE:	(802) 457-4322; (800) 791-8045
E-MAIL:	stanglin@sover.net
WEBSITE:	www.carriagehousewoodstock.com
ROOMS:	9 Rooms; Private baths
CHILDREN:	Children age 10 and older welcome
ANIMALS:	Not allowed; Resident cat
HANDICAPPED:	Not handicapped accessible
DIETARY NEEDS:	Will accommodate guests' special dietary needs

Pumpkin Chocolate Chip Muffins

Makes 12 Muffins

"This is my daughter's favorite muffin. The dark brown sugar makes them very moist." - Innkeeper, Carriage House of Woodstock Bed & Breakfast

- 1⅔ cups all-purpose flour
- ¾ teaspoon baking powder
- 1 teaspoon baking soda
- ½ teaspoon salt
- 2 teaspoons pumpkin pie spice
- 1 cup canned pumpkin
- ¼ cup evaporated milk
- 5⅓ tablespoons butter or shortening, softened
- 1 cup packed dark brown sugar
- 1 large egg
- 1⅓ cups semi-sweet chocolate chips

Preheat oven to 350°F. In a medium bowl, combine flour, baking powder, baking soda, salt, pumpkin pie spice; set aside. In a small bowl, combine pumpkin and evaporated milk. In a large bowl, cream together butter or shortening and sugar. Add egg and beat until fluffy. Alternately add flour and pumpkin mixtures to butter mixture, beating well after each addition. Stir in chocolate chips. Fill lightly greased or paper-lined muffin cups ⅔-full. Bake for 35-40 minutes.

Deacon Timothy Pratt

Step back in time in this magnificent, circa 1746, center chimney, Colonial bed & breakfast listed on the National Register of Historic Places. The Deacon Timothy Pratt is located in the charming, quintessential New England village of Old Saybrook, on a pretty, gas-lit main street in the heart of the historic and shopping districts.

The romantic guest rooms feature award-winning decor that combines the historical charm of yesteryear with the relaxing luxuries of today. Each room has a four-poster or canopy bed, Jacuzzi tub and fireplace.

INNKEEPERS:	Patricia McGregor & Shelley Nobile
ADDRESS:	325 Main Street
	Old Saybrook, Connecticut 06475
TELEPHONE:	(860) 395-1229; (800) 640-1195
E-MAIL:	shelley.nobile@snet.net
WEBSITE:	www.pratthouse.net
ROOMS:	7 Rooms; 1 Suite; Private baths
CHILDREN:	Children age 10 and older welcome
ANIMALS:	Not allowed
HANDICAPPED:	Handicapped accessible
DIETARY NEEDS:	Will accommodate guests' special dietary needs

Cappuccino Chocolate Chip Muffins

Makes 12 Muffins

"A great, tasty compliment to your morning coffee." - Innkeeper, Deacon Timothy Pratt Bed & Breakfast

1½	sticks butter, softened
1⅓	cups sugar
2	large eggs
2	teaspoons vanilla extract
¼	cup instant coffee powder
¼	cup Kahlúa or other coffee-flavored liqueur (optional)
3½	cups unsifted all-purpose flour
1	tablespoon baking powder
1	teaspoon salt
½	cup milk
1½	cups chocolate chips

Preheat oven to 350°F. Grease muffin cups. In a large bowl beat butter and sugar with a mixer on medium speed until light and fluffy. Beat in eggs, vanilla, instant coffee and Kahlúa until instant coffee is dissolved and Kahlúa is combined.

In a medium bowl, combine flour, baking powder and salt. Add flour mixture and milk alternately to butter mixture, beating just until combined. Fold in chocolate chips. Divide batter among muffin cups. Bake for 25-30 minutes, or until centers spring back when lightly pressed. Serve warm.

Colby Hill Inn

The Colby Hill Inn is a classic New England bed & breakfast country inn with 15 lovely guest rooms, acclaimed dining and warm hospitality. Chef Jeannine Carney invites you to enjoy the best of what New England and New Hampshire have to offer. Many items come from local suppliers who are proudly featured on the menu. This "cooking local" philosophy ensures that guests enjoy fresh, creative and seasonally prepared cuisine.

Dishes might include steamed Narragansett mussels or farm-raised Bonnie Brae venison with maple sugar rub and spiced rhubarb chutney.

INNKEEPERS:	Cyndi & Mason Cobb
ADDRESS:	3 The Oaks
	Henniker, New Hampshire 03242
TELEPHONE:	(603) 428-3281; (800) 531-0330
E-MAIL:	innkeeper@colbyhillinn.com
WEBSITE:	www.colbyhillinn.com
ROOMS:	13 Rooms; 2 Suites; Private baths
CHILDREN:	Children age 7 and older welcome
ANIMALS:	Not allowed
HANDICAPPED:	Limited; Call ahead
DIETARY NEEDS:	Will accommodate guests' special dietary needs

Sweet Potato Muffins or Bread

Makes 36 Muffins or 3 Loaves

"One of our guests' favorites!" - Innkeeper, Colby Hill Inn

2	cups mashed peeled, cooked sweet potatoes
1	cup vegetable oil
4	large eggs
1	cup water, rum or brandy (or a mixture of any or all)
1	teaspoon vanilla extract
3	cups sugar
3½	cups all-purpose flour
2	teaspoons baking soda
½	teaspoon salt
1	teaspoon cinnamon
1	cup raisins (optional)

Streusel topping:

¾	cup chopped nuts (walnuts or pecans are good)
¾	cup packed brown sugar
½	stick butter, melted
1½	teaspoons cinnamon

Preheat oven to 350°F. Grease muffin cups or 3 (9x5-inch) loaf pans. In a large bowl, combine sweet potatoes, oil, eggs, water and vanilla. In a medium bowl, combine flour, baking soda, salt and cinnamon; add to sweet potato mixture and stir until combined. Stir in raisins, if desired. Pour batter into muffin cups or loaf pans. Sprinkle topping over batter. Bake muffins for 30 minutes or loaves for 1 hour.

For the topping: Combine all topping ingredients until crumbly.

The Inn on Golden Pond

The Inn on Golden Pond is located on 50 wooded acres, giving it a rural feel, yet it is a short drive to virtually all of the state's major attractions. Nearby is Squam Lake, the setting for the classic film "On Golden Pond." There are miles of open waterway to sail, motor, paddle or swim in. The inn is minutes from the Squam range and is nestled in the foothills of the White Mountains, making it a great spot for hikers and skiers alike.

Breakfast is most often served buffet style. Sit and enjoy the beautiful view. Guests have seen deer, moose and even black bears while enjoying breakfast.

INNKEEPERS:	Bill & Bonnie Webb
ADDRESS:	Route 3
	Holderness, New Hampshire 03245
TELEPHONE:	(603) 968-7269
E-MAIL:	innongp@lr.net
WEBSITE:	www.innongoldenpond.com
ROOMS:	6 Rooms; 2 Suites; Private baths
CHILDREN:	Children age 12 and older welcome
ANIMALS:	Not allowed; Resident dogs
HANDICAPPED:	Not handicapped accessible
DIETARY NEEDS:	Will accommodate guests' special dietary needs

Flat-Top Orange Date Muffins

Makes 12 Muffins

Rind of 1 orange
1 orange, quartered and pith removed
½ cup orange juice
1 stick unsalted butter, softened
1 large egg, lightly beaten
½ cup chopped dates
1½ cups all-purpose flour
1 teaspoon baking soda
¾ cup sugar
1 teaspoon baking powder
Dash of salt

Preheat oven to 400°F. Chop orange rind in a food processor. Add orange quarters, orange juice, butter, egg and dates; chop and set aside. Sift together flour, baking soda, sugar, baking powder and salt into a large bowl. Add orange mixture to flour mixture; stir just until moistened. Divide batter among greased muffin cups. Bake for 20-25 minutes.

The Knoll

The Knoll is a spacious, circa 1910 home of country Tudor design. All floors are wood with many Oriental rugs scattered about. The inn is a peaceful retreat with 17 acres of farmland and forest and an acre of lawn in front of the house. Breakfast is served in the paneled, formal dining room.

Within a few minutes drive of the Knoll, you can reach any of the five colleges located in western Massachusetts – Smith, Amherst, Mt. Holyoke, University of Massachusetts and Hampshire.

INNKEEPERS:	Leona (Lee) Lesko
ADDRESS:	230 North Main Street
	Florence (Northhampton), Massachusetts 01062
TELEPHONE:	(413) 584-8164
E-MAIL:	theknoll@crocker.com
WEBSITE:	www.crocker.com/~theknoll
ROOMS:	4 Rooms; Private & shared baths
CHILDREN:	Children age 12 and older welcome
ANIMALS:	Not allowed
HANDICAPPED:	Not handicapped accessible
DIETARY NEEDS:	Will accommodate guests' special dietary needs

Apple Muffins

Makes 12 Muffins

1¼	cups all-purpose flour
¾	cup sugar
¼	cup quick-cooking rolled oats
1½	teaspoons baking powder
½	teaspoon salt
¾	teaspoon cinnamon
¼	teaspoon nutmeg
2	large eggs
⅓	cup vegetable oil
2	cups chopped peeled apples
1½	tablespoons water
½	cup chopped walnuts

Preheat oven to 375°F. In a large bowl, combine flour, sugar, oats, baking powder, salt, cinnamon and nutmeg. In a medium bowl, combine eggs, oil, apples, water and walnuts; add to flour mixture and stir until flour mixture is moistened. Pour batter into greased or paper-lined muffin cups and bake for 15-20 minutes.

The Benjamin Prescott Inn

Remember your Grandmother's house? Do you recall the kitchen? Grandmother was always there – she would be baking a pie or pulling freshly made cookies from the oven. When you walked outside, the cows would "moo" at you and there was always a grassy hill to climb. Well, that's what life is like at the Benjamin Prescott Inn.

Time travel back to the mid-19th century. Immerse yourself in all that was good about that era. Draw beauty from the Monadnock region and find solace within the walls of the inn.

INNKEEPERS:	Bob & Alice Seidel
ADDRESS:	Route 124 East, 433 Turnpike Road
	Jaffrey, New Hampshire 03452
TELEPHONE:	(603) 532-6637; (888) 950-6637
E-MAIL:	innkeeper@benjaminprescottinn.com
WEBSITE:	www.benjaminprescottinn.com
ROOMS:	7 Rooms; 3 Suites; Private baths
CHILDREN:	Children age 12 and older welcome
ANIMALS:	Not allowed; Resident dog
HANDICAPPED:	Not handicapped accessible
DIETARY NEEDS:	Will accommodate guests' special dietary needs

Blueberry Cream Muffins

Makes 18 to 20 Muffins

2	large eggs
1	cup sugar
½	cup vegetable oil
½	teaspoon vanilla extract
2	cups all-purpose flour
½	teaspoon salt
½	teaspoon baking soda
1	teaspoon baking powder
1	cup sour cream
1	cup fresh or frozen (thawed) blueberries

Topping:
2	tablespoons sugar
1	teaspoon cinnamon

Preheat oven to 400°F. Spray muffin cups with non-stick cooking spray. In a large bowl, beat eggs. Beat in sugar. Beat in oil and vanilla. In a medium bowl, combine flour, salt, baking soda and baking powder. Alternately mix flour mixture and sour cream into egg mixture. Gently fold in blueberries. Pour batter into muffin cups. Sprinkle topping over batter in muffin cups. Bake for 20 minutes.

For the topping: Combine sugar and cinnamon.

Arbor Rose

At one time, there were six mills on the Kampoosa Brook, all built between 1782 and 1822. They included a gristmill, distillery, woolen factory, chair factory, sawmill and a trip hammer shop. The sawmill, which was in operation until the 1930s, still stands and houses some of the Arbor Rose's guests within its old post-and-beam construction.

The inn is committed to serving "tasty, fresh, local and homemade food." Guests return just for their favorite muffins! Breakfast includes something home-baked, homemade granola or cereal and entrées on the weekends.

INNKEEPERS:	Christina Alsop
ADDRESS:	8 Yale Hill Road
	Stockbridge, Massachusetts 01262
TELEPHONE:	(413) 298-4744
E-MAIL:	innkeeper@arborrose.com
WEBSITE:	www.arborrose.com
ROOMS:	7 Rooms; 1 Suite; Private baths
CHILDREN:	Welcome
ANIMALS:	Call ahead; Resident dog & cat in farmhouse
HANDICAPPED:	Not handicapped accessible
DIETARY NEEDS:	Will accommodate guests' special dietary needs

Apple or Carrot Bran Muffins

Makes 14 Muffins

1½	cups whole-wheat flour
1	cup unbleached all-purpose flour
1	cup bran
1	cup coconut
1½	teaspoons baking soda
1	teaspoon baking powder

Pinch of salt

⅔	cup sugar
1	teaspoon cinnamon
2	eggs, beaten
⅔	cup vegetable oil
¼	cup honey, warmed slightly (aids mixing)
2	tablespoons molasses (if making carrot muffins), warmed slightly
⅔	cup vanilla yogurt
1	cup buttermilk
2½	cups grated peeled Granny Smith apple or carrot
1¼	cups raisins

Preheat oven to 325°F. In a medium bowl, combine whole-wheat and all-purpose flour, bran, coconut, baking soda, baking powder, salt, sugar and cinnamon. In a large bowl, combine eggs, vegetable oil, honey, molasses (if making carrot muffins), yogurt, buttermilk, apples or carrots and raisins. Add flour mixture to apple or carrot mixture; stir until combined. Pour batter into greased or paper-lined muffin cups. Bake for 20-25 minutes. Let stand for 5 minutes before removing muffins from cups.

Coffee Cakes, Scones, Granola & Oatmeal

Blueberry Sour Cream Cake 49

Cranberry Apple Coffee Cake 51

Maine Apple Cake 53

Applesauce Currant Cake 55

Blueberry Sage Scones 57

Maple Oatmeal Scones 59

Apple Walnut Cream Scones 61

Cranberry Scones 63

Hill Farm Granola 65

Irish Oatmeal 67

Coffee Cakes, Scones, Granola & Oatmeal

Captain Lindsey House Inn

Nestled amongst the historic seaport buildings of Rockland, the circa 1837 Captain Lindsey House Inn offers a quiet, comfortable and cozy retreat from your day's activities. One of Rockland's first inns, it is located downtown, within easy walking distance of shops, museums and the busy waterfront.

The Captain Lindsey House Inn is reminiscent of a lovely roadside English inn or a Sea Captain's home in the early 1800s, filled with artifacts and furnishings from all parts of the world.

INNKEEPERS:	Cindy D'Ambrosio & Vivian Caine
ADDRESS:	5 Lindsey Street
	Rockland, Maine 04841
TELEPHONE:	(207) 596-7950; (800) 523-2145
E-MAIL:	lindsey@midcoast.com
WEBSITE:	www.lindseyhouse.com
ROOMS:	9 Rooms; Private baths
CHILDREN:	Welcome
ANIMALS:	Not allowed
HANDICAPPED:	Handicapped accessible
DIETARY NEEDS:	Will accommodate guests' special dietary needs

Blueberry Sour Cream Cake

Makes 8 Servings

"We grow the best wild blueberries in Maine. They are small and very tasty. During the season, in late July and August, we try to use our blueberries as much as possible." ~ Innkeeper, Captain Lindsey House Inn

1½	cups all-purpose flour
½	cup sugar
1	stick butter, softened
1	egg
1½	teaspoons baking powder
1	teaspoon vanilla extract
1	quart fresh blueberries

Topping:

½	cup sugar
1	teaspoon vanilla extract
2	cups sour cream
2	egg yolks

Preheat oven to 350°F. Combine flour, sugar, butter, egg, baking powder, vanilla and blueberries; pat into a 9-inch springform pan. Pour topping over batter. Bake for 75 minutes, or until a toothpick inserted in center comes out clean.

For the topping: Combine all topping ingredients.

Lakeshore Inn

Located in Rockland, the recently renovated Lakeshore Inn is an elegant bed & breakfast nestled against Dodge Mountain and overlooking Lake Chickawaukie. Each of the distinctly decorated rooms has a view of the lake. Relax in a nearly rural setting two miles from the beach and in close proximity to the attractions of Midcoast Maine, including Camden, the Farnsworth Museum and the Owls Head Transportation Museum.

"Everything was done with elegance and grace and to perfection. Not a stone left unturned. Hope to make it a tradition." ~ Guest, Lakeshore Inn

INNKEEPERS:	Pat & Jim Mason
ADDRESS:	184 Lakeview Drive
	Rockland, Maine 04841
TELEPHONE:	(207) 594-4209; (866) 540-8800
E-MAIL:	info@lakeshorebb.com
WEBSITE:	www.lakeshorebb.com
ROOMS:	4 Rooms; Private baths
CHILDREN:	Children age 12 and older welcome
ANIMALS:	Not allowed
HANDICAPPED:	Not handicapped accessible
DIETARY NEEDS:	Will accommodate guests' special dietary needs

Cranberry Apple Coffee Cake

Makes 10 Servings

"This simple coffee cake is such a hit with our guests! I frequently receive thank you notes and emails from guests who can't believe how easy it is and how many compliments they receive when they serve it." ~ Innkeeper, Lakeshore Inn

1	(18¼-ounce) box yellow cake mix
1	(21-ounce) can cranberry-apple pie filling
4	large eggs, beaten
⅔	cup all-purpose flour
½	cup sugar
5	tablespoons butter, softened
1½	teaspoons cinnamon
⅔	cup powdered sugar
2	tablespoons milk

Preheat oven to 350°F. Combine cake mix, pie filling and eggs; mix well and pour into a greased 9x13-inch baking pan. Combine flour, sugar, butter and cinnamon; blend with a pastry blender until moist and crumbly. Sprinkle flour mixture on top of batter.

Bake for 45 minutes. Cool cake in pan. While cake is cooling, combine powdered sugar and milk. When cake is cool, drizzle powdered sugar mixture over top of cake.

1794 Watchtide by the Sea

If you are searching for the sweet smell of crisp, clean, fresh salt air mixed with the bouquet of flowering trees, wildflowers, pines and all the other things in life that seem to be more and more a part of the past, look no further than 1794 Watchtide by the Sea. This historic, 18th century inn became well known in the early 20th century as the College Club Inn, hosting presidential wives with Eleanor Roosevelt making frequent visits.

"To enjoy a stay at Watchtide is to be among those lucky enough to experience a bit of heaven on earth." ~ Karen K. Snyder, Travel Journalist

INNKEEPERS:	Nancy-Linn Nellis
ADDRESS:	190 West Main
	Searsport, Maine, 04974
TELEPHONE:	(207) 548-6575; (800) 698-6575
E-MAIL:	stay@watchtide.com
WEBSITE:	www.watchtide.com
ROOMS:	3 Rooms; 2 Suites; Private baths
CHILDREN:	Children age 10 and older welcome
ANIMALS:	Not allowed
HANDICAPPED:	Not handicapped accessible
DIETARY NEEDS:	Will accommodate guests' special dietary needs

Maine Apple Cake

Makes 1 Cake

"We serve this as a breakfast bread." - Innkeeper, 1794 Watchtide by the Sea

2	large Granny Smith apples, peeled
1¾	cups pure Maine maple syrup
3	large eggs
1	cup canola oil
1	teaspoon vanilla extract
1	teaspoon baking soda
1	teaspoon salt
2	teaspoons cinnamon
2	cups all-purpose flour
1	cup sweetened dried cranberries (or craisins)
1	cup chopped walnuts

Powdered sugar, for garnish

Preheat oven to 375°F. Grease a 9x13-inch baking pan. Halve apples lengthwise and thinly slice them lengthwise. Line baking pan with apples.

In a large bowl, combine baking soda, salt, cinnamon and flour. In a small bowl, combine maple syrup, eggs and oil. Stir in vanilla. Add maple syrup mixture to flour mixture; mix well. Stir in cranberries and walnuts. Pour batter evenly over apples in pan.

Bake for 45-50 minutes, or until a toothpick inserted in center comes out clean. Dust warm cake with powdered sugar to serve.

The Whipple-Tree

The Whipple-Tree is a newly-built bed & breakfast located in the beautiful and historic town of Newbury. Perched on a mountain, the views are breathtaking and the surroundings are nature's best! In the morning, savor Belgian waffles with your choice of toppings, eggs to order, quiches, omelets, crêpes or pancakes with locally-made maple syrup.

Enjoy fly fishing, hiking, biking, golf, cross-country skiing, snowshoeing, skating, hot-air ballooning, antique and crafts shopping, a visit to a local alpaca farm and spectacular drives during Vermont's famed fall foliage season.

INNKEEPERS:	William & Carol Bailey
ADDRESS:	487 Stevens Place
	Newbury, Vermont 05081
TELEPHONE:	(802) 429-2076; (800) 466-4097
E-MAIL:	whiptree@together.net
WEBSITE:	www.whipple-tree.com
ROOMS:	6 Rooms; Private baths
CHILDREN:	Children welcome
ANIMALS:	Dogs welcome; call ahead
HANDICAPPED:	Handicapped accessible
DIETARY NEEDS:	Will accommodate guests' special dietary needs

Applesauce Currant Cake

Makes 8 to 10 Servings

"Although this is a cake, I serve it for breakfast with a dish of my homemade applesauce to the delight of my guests. As they say, this is a keeper." - Innkeeper, The Whipple-Tree Bed & Breakfast

1	cup packed light brown sugar
1	cup white sugar
¾	cup vegetable oil
2	large eggs
Pinch of salt	
1	tablespoon vanilla extract
2	cups applesauce
3	cups all-purpose flour
2	teaspoons baking soda
1	teaspoon ground cloves
1½	teaspoons cinnamon
1	teaspoon nutmeg
½	teaspoon ground ginger
1	cup currants
1	cup chopped nuts (optional)

Powdered sugar, for garnish

Preheat oven to 325°F. Grease and flour a Bundt pan. In a large bowl, cream brown sugar, white sugar and oil. Add eggs, vanilla and applesauce. Sift together flour, baking soda, cloves, cinnamon, nutmeg and ginger into a medium bowl; add to sugar mixture and mix well. Stir in currants and nuts. Pour batter into pan and bake for 75 minutes. Cool for 10 minutes, then turn out onto a wire rack and cool completely. Sprinkle with powdered sugar to serve.

Hartwell House Inn

The Hartwell House Inn is an elegant, antique-filled inn situated at the entrance of Perkins Cove, where lobster boats depart each morning and shops and restaurants overlook the ocean. The scenic Marginal Way footpath, which winds along the rugged coast, is only moments away.

The inn's acclaimed SW Swan Bistro features local, organic and seasonal ingredients. Offerings might include brandied pumpkin, tomato and onion soup with gruyère cheese and minced prosciutto; oven-steamed Arctic Char fillet; and souffléd brioche bread pudding with vanilla whiskey sauce.

INNKEEPERS:	Paul & Gail Koehler
ADDRESS:	312 Shore Road
	Ogunquit, Maine 03907
TELEPHONE:	(207) 646-7210; (800) 235-8883
E-MAIL:	info@hartwellhouseinn.com
WEBSITE:	www.hartwellhouseinn.com
ROOMS:	13 Rooms; 3 Suites; Private baths
CHILDREN:	Children age 16 and older welcome
ANIMALS:	Not allowed
HANDICAPPED:	Not handicapped accessible
DIETARY NEEDS:	Will accommodate guests' special dietary needs

Blueberry Sage Scones

Makes 24 Scones

"Capturing the bountiful harvest of local Maine blueberries, these scones are delightful for breakfast and afternoon tea alike – the perfect combination of sweet and savory." ~ Innkeeper, Hartwell House Inn

5¼	cups all-purpose flour
¾	cup plus 1 tablespoon sugar
2	tablespoons plus 1½ teaspoons baking powder
2¼	teaspoons salt
2½	sticks butter, chilled and cubed
6-7	ounces dried blueberries
1	tablespoon finely chopped fresh sage
2	cups plus 1½ tablespoons heavy cream

Preheat oven to 350°F. Sift together flour, sugar, baking powder and salt into a large bowl or the bowl of a stand mixer. Add butter and mix with a mixer just until pea-sized clumps form. Add blueberries, sage and 2 cups of heavy cream; mix just until combined.

Scoop dough with an ice cream scoop onto a cookie sheet or roll out ⅞-inch thick and cut with a 3-inch biscuit cutter or a glass. Brush with remaining 1½ tablespoons of heavy cream. Bake for 10 minutes, or until golden brown. Cool for 10 minutes before serving.

Maine Stay Inn & Cottages

The Maine Stay Inn at the Melville Walker House is a romantic bed & breakfast inn offering historic lodging, New England hospitality and the unsurpassed beauty of the rocky coast of Maine. Listed on the National Register of Historic Places, the inn offers a charming and comfortable ambiance within the quaint seaside village of Kennebunkport.

The inn is just a short stroll along tree-lined streets to the fine shops, galleries and restaurants of Dock Square. Nature trails, sandy beaches and quiet coves provide the tranquility to soothe the soul.

INNKEEPERS:	George & Janice Yankowski
ADDRESS:	34 Maine Street
	Kennebunkport, Maine 04046
TELEPHONE:	(207) 967-2117; (800) 950-2117
E-MAIL:	innkeeper@mainestayinn.com
WEBSITE:	www.mainestayinn.com
ROOMS:	4 Rooms; 3 Suites; 10 Cottages; Private baths
CHILDREN:	Welcome
ANIMALS:	Not allowed
HANDICAPPED:	Not handicapped accessible
DIETARY NEEDS:	Will accommodate guests' special dietary needs

Maple Oatmeal Scones

Makes 15 Scones

"This is one of our most popular items, especially in fall." ~ Innkeeper, Maine Stay Inn & Cottages

2	sticks butter, chilled and diced
2	tablespoons sugar, plus extra for garnish
2	eggs plus 1 egg, separated
½	cup plus 1 teaspoon maple syrup
1¾	cups all-purpose flour
½	cup whole-wheat flour
1	teaspoon salt
1	tablespoon baking powder
2	tablespoons plain yogurt
½	cup quick-cooking oats

Preheat oven to 375°F. In a large bowl, beat butter, sugar, eggs, egg yolk and ½ cup of maple syrup with a mixer until fluffy. In a medium bowl, combine all-purpose and whole-wheat flour, salt and baking powder. Add flour mixture to butter mixture; mix thoroughly by hand. Stir in yogurt and oats.

Scoop dough with an ice cream scoop filled ¾-full onto an ungreased cookie sheet. Beat egg white and combine with 1 teaspoon of maple syrup; brush on tops of scones. Sprinkle with sugar. Bake for 15-20 minutes, until golden brown.

The Arbor Inn

The Arbor Inn is a beautifully decorated home offering guests a comfortable, quiet and relaxing refuge. The inn is within walking distance of Wallis Sands Beach of Rye and only a few minutes drive to historic Portsmouth, Strawberry Banke Museum, theaters, shopping, a delicious array of restaurants, golf, state parks and harbor boat cruises.

Enjoy spectacular gourmet breakfasts and an afternoon treat of handmade pastries made by innkeeper Joanne Nichols, an award-winning pastry chef.

INNKEEPERS:	Joanne Nichols
ADDRESS:	400 Brackett Road
	Rye, New Hampshire 03870
TELEPHONE:	(603) 431-7010
E-MAIL:	arbor@gsinet.net
WEBSITE:	www.arborinn.com
ROOMS:	4 Rooms; 1 Suite; Private baths
CHILDREN:	Children welcome
ANIMALS:	Not allowed
HANDICAPPED:	Not handicapped accessible
DIETARY NEEDS:	Will accommodate guests' special dietary needs

Apple Walnut Cream Scones

Makes 12 Scones

"These scones will melt in your mouth!" ~ Innkeeper, The Arbor Inn

1	tablespoon butter plus 1 stick unsalted butter, chilled and cubed
1	large apple, chopped into ½-inch chunks
3	tablespoons packed light brown sugar
1	teaspoon cinnamon
2½	cups all-purpose flour
2	teaspoons baking powder
1	teaspoon baking soda
½	cup sugar
½	cup sour cream
1	large egg
¾	cup heavy cream
½	cup chopped walnuts

Maple fondant:

2	cups powdered sugar
1	tablespoon maple extract
Water	

Preheat oven to 400°F. Melt 1 tablespoon of butter with brown sugar and cinnamon in a skillet over medium heat. Add apples and cook until softened; set aside and cool. In a food processor, process flour, baking powder, baking soda and sugar until well blended. Add cubed unsalted butter; process until crumbly. Mix in sour cream and egg. With motor running, pour cream into feed tube and process just until dough comes together. Stir in walnuts and apple mixture by hand.

Form dough into a ball, wrap in plastic wrap and chill for 1 hour. On a floured surface, roll dough into a ball. Cut ball into 12 pie-shaped wedges. Put scones on a parchment paper-lined cookie sheet. Bake scones for 12-15 minutes, until golden brown and tops spring back slightly. Drizzle fondant over scones. Let stand just until fondant is set. Serve warm.

For the fondant: Mix powdered sugar and maple extract. Add water, a few drops at a time, until sugar is slightly dissolved and mixture is very thick.

The Seagull Inn

On Marblehead Neck, casual elegance welcomes guests to the century-old Seagull Inn. Glorious gardens in summer and spectacular views from the decks throughout the year make every season special here. Luxurious suites, most with ocean and harbor views, complement the seaside setting. Each suite has been totally restored with cherry floors, Shaker furniture and original paintings.

In the morning, enjoy a view of the harbor with a breakfast of homemade granola, muffins and breads, fresh coffee, bagels and smoked salmon.

INNKEEPERS:	Ruth & Skip Sigler
ADDRESS:	106 Harbor Avenue
	Marblehead, Massachusetts 01945
TELEPHONE:	(781) 631-1893
E-MAIL:	host@seagullinn.com
WEBSITE:	www.seagullinn.com
ROOMS:	3 Suites; Private baths
CHILDREN:	Children welcome
ANIMALS:	Dogs welcome; call ahead
HANDICAPPED:	Not handicapped accessible
DIETARY NEEDS:	Will accommodate guests' special dietary needs

Cranberry Scones

Makes 16 to 20 Scones

3	cups all-purpose flour
4	teaspoons baking powder
½	teaspoon baking soda
½	teaspoon salt
½	cup sugar
2	sticks unsalted butter, chilled and diced
3	large eggs
⅔	cup buttermilk or plain yogurt
1	cup frozen or fresh cranberries, each snipped in half with scissors
1	teaspoon freshly grated orange zest

Preheat oven to 350°F. Process flour, baking powder, baking soda, salt, sugar and butter in a food processor until mixture is consistency of cornmeal.

Beat eggs and buttermilk with a mixer. Beat in flour mixture until a soft dough forms. Fold in cranberries and orange zest. Scoop dough with an ice cream scoop onto an ungreased cookie sheet. Bake scones for about 20 minutes, until golden.

Note: This dough freezes well and yields fresh-baked treats with minimal time in the morning. Simply scoop dough onto a cookie sheet, lightly cover with plastic wrap and freeze. When frozen, seal in plastic freezer bags. When ready to bake, place frozen dough on an ungreased cookie sheet and bake immediately in a preheated 350°F oven for about 25 minutes, until golden.

Hill Farm Inn

The Hill Farm Inn offers five guest rooms on the second floor of the 1830 main inn and six rooms in the 1790 guest house. Each room is decorated to capture the spirit and charm of a New England farmhouse. Visit the friendly farm animals, explore two and one-half miles of walking trails or just sit on the porch and enjoy the surroundings.

In summer, there is access to the Appalachian Trail in the nearby Green Mountain National Forest. In winter, there are myriad cross-country ski trails and Stratton Mountain and Bromley Mountain are close by.

INNKEEPERS:	Lisa & Al Gray
ADDRESS:	458 Hill Farm Road
	Arlington, Vermont 05250
TELEPHONE:	(802) 375-2269; (800) 882-2545
E-MAIL:	stay@hillfarminn.com
WEBSITE:	www.hillfarminn.com
ROOMS:	5 Rooms; 6 Suites; 4 Cottages; Private baths
CHILDREN:	Children welcome
ANIMALS:	Not allowed; Resident goats, sheep, chickens, dog
HANDICAPPED:	Not handicapped accessible
DIETARY NEEDS:	Will accommodate guests' special dietary needs

Hill Farm Granola

Makes About 3½ Cups

"This granola has no added fat or oil. It's been a Hill Farm favorite for many years." ~ Innkeeper, Hill Farm Inn

1	cup old-fashioned rolled oats
⅓	cup chopped nuts
⅓	cup wheat germ
⅓	cup sesame seeds
⅓	cup sunflower seeds
⅓	cup shredded coconut
⅓	cup banana chips
⅓	cup dried cranberries
¼	cup packed brown sugar

Put oats and nuts in a large, heavy skillet over low heat; cook for 5 minutes, stirring often. Add wheat germ, sesame seeds, sunflower seeds, coconut, banana chips and dried cranberries; cook for 10 minutes. Add brown sugar and cook for 2 minutes longer. Transfer granola to a bowl and cool. When granola is completely cool, store in an air-tight container.

Note: This granola can be frozen for up to 3 months.

Maple Manor

Maple Manor is a 250-acre estate located in Vermont's Northeast Kingdom. Situated at the end of a driveway lined with 100-year-old maples, the house overlooks nearby Lake Parker. Decorated in Victorian style, the restored farmhouse is luxurious and comfortable. The property has maple trees, open meadows and the rolling hills for which Vermont is known. It is the perfect setting for privacy, relaxation and romance.

Stroll or snowshoe around the property, explore the gardens, barn and pool or just relax in the house and enjoy Southern-style hospitality.

INNKEEPERS:	Sandra Hazen
ADDRESS:	77 Maple Lane
	West Glover, Vermont 05875
TELEPHONE:	(802) 525-9591
E-MAIL:	mplmnr@together.net
WEBSITE:	www.maple-manor.com
ROOMS:	3 Rooms; Private baths
CHILDREN:	Children age 10 and older welcome
ANIMALS:	Not allowed
HANDICAPPED:	Not handicapped accessible
DIETARY NEEDS:	Will accommodate guests' special dietary needs

Irish Oatmeal

Makes 4 Servings

"Be sure to stir before eating – luscious treasures can be found in the bottom of the bowl." ~ Innkeeper, Maple Manor Bed & Breakfast

2	cups water
¼	teaspoon salt
½	stick butter
2	cups old-fashioned rolled oats
⅓	cup light corn syrup
¼	cup brandy
1	cup golden raisins
½	cup heavy cream, divided
¼	cup packed light brown sugar, divided

Fresh blueberries, for serving
Whipped cream, for serving

Bring water and salt to a boil in a medium saucepan. Add butter and oats; lower heat to medium and simmer for 6-10 minutes, until tender.

Heat corn syrup and brandy in a small saucepan over medium heat. Add raisins and simmer for 3-5 minutes; remove from heat and cool.

When ready to serve, drain raisins. Put 2 tablespoons of cream, 1 tablespoon of brown sugar and 1 tablespoon of raisins in each of 4 bowls. Add steaming hot oatmeal. Top with blueberries and/or whipped cream.

Pancakes & Waffles

Carmel Apple Pumpkin Pancakes 71

Gingerbread Pancakes 73

Pancakes Verona 75

Lemon Blueberry Pancakes 77

Oatmeal Apple Pancakes 79

Four-Berry Pancakes 81

Sour Cream, Peach & Blueberry Pancakes 83

Yogurt Pancakes 85

Apple Clafouti 87

Maple-Apple Waffles with Ben & Jerry's Ice Cream 89

Wicked Good Belgian Waffles with Maine Blueberry Compote 91

Apple Waffles with Apple Cider Syrup 93

Orange Waffles 95

Pancakes & Waffles

The Siebeness Inn

The Siebeness ("seven S's") is named for the seven "S" turns on Stowe's famous Nosedive Trail. The inn has been welcoming guests for over 50 years in a setting of over 70 acres of pristine mountain meadows. Lovingly restored with modern amenities, it provides outstanding food and an atmosphere of romance, relaxation and rejuvenation.

Innkeeper and award-winning chef Toni Ruffing creates decadent country breakfasts to please any palate. No wonder *Yankee Magazine* picked the inn as "one of the outstanding reasons to visit New England!"

INNKEEPERS:	Toni & Will Ruffing
ADDRESS:	3681 Mountain Road
	Stowe, Vermont 05672
TELEPHONE:	(802) 253-9232; (800) 426-9001
E-MAIL:	siebeness@aol.com
WEBSITE:	www.siebeness.com
ROOMS:	10 Rooms; 2 Suites; Private baths
CHILDREN:	Children age 12 and older welcome
ANIMALS:	Not allowed; Resident dog
HANDICAPPED:	Not handicapped accessible
DIETARY NEEDS:	Will accommodate guests' special dietary needs

Caramel Apple Pumpkin Pancakes

Makes 10 to 12 Servings

"This is what fall in Vermont is all about!" ~ *Innkeeper, The Siebeness, A Romantic Country Inn*

Pancakes:
- 1   (32-ounce) package pancake mix
- 1   cup canned pumpkin
- 2   teaspoons cinnamon
- ½   cup sugar
- ¼   teaspoon nutmeg

Caramel apples:
- 1   cup packed brown sugar
- ½   stick butter
- 4   apples, peeled and thinly sliced

For the pancakes: Prepare pancake mix according to package directions. Add nutmeg, sugar, pumpkin and cinnamon; mix gently. Cook pancakes on a greased, preheated griddle or skillet until browned on both sides. Serve topped with caramel apples.

For the caramel apples: Combine butter and brown sugar in a saucepan over low heat. Add apples and cook until sugar caramelizes with apples.

Sugar Hill Inn

The Sugar Hill Inn was built in 1789 as a small farmhouse for one of the early settling families in the Sugar Hill area of New Hampshire. Nestled into a hillside and set on 16 acres of woodlands, rolling lawns and well-tended gardens, the Sugar Hill Inn is surrounded by the beauty and tranquility of New Hampshire's White Mountains.

Rooms are bright and inviting, and many have views overlooking the garden. A recent addition to the inn includes two luxury suites. Each features a fireplace, whirlpool bath and private deck.

INNKEEPERS:	Judy & Orlo Coots
ADDRESS:	Scenic Route 117
	Sugar Hill, New Hampshire 03585
TELEPHONE:	(603) 823-5621; (800) 548-4748
E-MAIL:	info@sugarhillinn.com
WEBSITE:	www.sugarhillinn.com
ROOMS:	9 Rooms; 6 Cottages; Private baths
CHILDREN:	Welcome
ANIMALS:	Not allowed
HANDICAPPED:	Not handicapped accessible
DIETARY NEEDS:	Will accommodate guests' special dietary needs

Gingerbread Pancakes

Makes 6 to 10 Servings

1	cup whole-wheat flour
1	cup all-purpose flour
¼	teaspoon nutmeg
¼	teaspoon ground ginger
½	teaspoon salt
1	tablespoon baking powder
½	teaspoon cinnamon
2	tablespoons packed brown sugar
½	cup molasses
2	eggs, separated
3	tablespoons butter, melted
1	cup milk

New Hampshire maple syrup, for serving
Freshly whipped cream, for serving

In a large bowl, combine whole-wheat and all-purpose flour, nutmeg, ginger, salt, baking powder, cinnamon and brown sugar. In a small bowl, combine molasses, egg yolks, butter and milk. In a medium bowl, beat egg whites until stiff. Gently fold molasses mixture into egg whites. Gently stir egg white mixture into flour mixture. Cook pancakes on a preheated, greased griddle or skillet until golden brown on both sides. Serve with maple syrup and whipped cream.

Silver Fox Farm

Woodstock has long been known as one of America's most beautiful villages and is one of the most sought after travel destinations in New England. Silver Fox Farm sits on a knoll among century-old hardwood forests in a quaint hamlet listed on the National Register of Historic Places. With just four rooms, the innkeepers are able to provide superb service and hospitality to the discerning traveler.

Guests sometimes sit for hours around the large, candlelit table enjoying the crackle of burning logs from the massive stone fireplace.

INNKEEPERS:	Christine DeLuca
ADDRESS:	7504 Happy Valley Road
	Woodstock, Vermont 05091
TELEPHONE:	(802) 457-5864
E-MAIL:	silverfoxfarm@hotmail.com
WEBSITE:	www.silverfoxfarmofvermont.com
ROOMS:	3 Rooms; 1 Suite; Private baths
CHILDREN:	Children welcome
ANIMALS:	Welcome; Resident dogs, horses, birds
HANDICAPPED:	Not handicapped accessible
DIETARY NEEDS:	Will accommodate guests' special dietary needs

Pancakes Verona

Makes 4 to 6 Servings

"These light-as-air pancakes taste great and our guests just love them!" - Innkeeper, Silver Fox Farm

6	large eggs, separated
2	cups cottage cheese
¼	cup vegetable oil
2	tablespoons maple syrup or sugar
½	teaspoon salt
4	teaspoons fresh lemon juice
4	teaspoons baking powder
1	cup all-purpose flour

Butter, for serving
Maple syrup, for serving

In a blender, blend egg yolks, cottage cheese, oil, maple syrup, salt, lemon juice, baking powder and flour; transfer to a bowl. In a separate bowl, beat egg whites until stiff. Fold egg whites into batter. Make pancakes using about 3 tablespoons of batter per pancake. Cook pancakes on a lightly buttered or oiled griddle or skillet over medium heat until golden brown on both sides. Serve with butter and maple syrup.

Rock Ledge Manor

Rock Ledge Manor is a gambrel-roofed inn with traditional wraparound porch overlooking the Atlantic Ocean and just south of Wallis Sands and Rye State Beach. The inn, built between 1840 and 1880 as part of a major seaside resort, has a style that is pure Victorian gingerbread. From the porch, watch as lobstermen haul in their catch and sailboats cruise by on their way from Portsmouth and Rye Harbor to the Isles of Shoals.

Take scenic walks along the shoreline and enjoy the picturesque sunrise and sunset. Or, relax in an Adirondack chair while sipping a cool beverage.

INNKEEPERS:	Paula Klkane & Phyllis Klkane
ADDRESS:	1413 Ocean Boulevard
	Rye, New Hampshire 03870
TELEPHONE:	(603) 431-1413
E-MAIL:	info@rockledgemanor.com
WEBSITE:	www.rockledgemanor.com
ROOMS:	2 Rooms; 1 Suite; Private baths
CHILDREN:	Children age 10 and older welcome
ANIMALS:	Not allowed; Resident dogs
HANDICAPPED:	Not handicapped accessible
DIETARY NEEDS:	Will accommodate guests' special dietary needs

Lemon Blueberry Pancakes

Makes 6 to 8 Servings

2   cups Stonewall Kitchen pancake mix, or other favorite pancake mix
2   eggs
1   tablespoon vanilla extract
Grated zest of 1 lemon
1   teaspoon fresh lemon juice
1   cup blueberries, preferably fresh

In a bowl, combine all ingredients, except blueberries. Fold in blueberries. Cook pancakes on a preheated, greased griddle or skillet until golden brown on both sides.

Maine Stay Inn & Cottages

The Maine Stay Inn, built in 1860, is a former sea captain's home that offers the grace and splendor of a bygone era. Choose the Victorian romance of a 19th century inn room or the private intimacy of an English country cottage suite. Relax around a cozy fire or enjoy a Jacuzzi tub.

Awaken to a sumptuous breakfast served in the dining room, or have your meal delivered to your private cottage suite in a wicker basket. In the afternoon, tea is served on the sunny porch in summer or around a cozy fire on cooler days.

INNKEEPERS:	George & Janice Yankowski
ADDRESS:	34 Maine Street
	Kennebunkport, Maine 04046
TELEPHONE:	(207) 967-2117; (800) 950-2117
E-MAIL:	innkeeper@mainestayinn.com
WEBSITE:	www.mainestayinn.com
ROOMS:	4 Rooms; 3 Suites; 10 Cottages; Private baths
CHILDREN:	Welcome
ANIMALS:	Not allowed
HANDICAPPED:	Not handicapped accessible
DIETARY NEEDS:	Will accommodate guests' special dietary needs

Oatmeal Apple Pancakes

Makes 12 to 18 Pancakes

"Serve with maple syrup or hot applesauce for a great treat on a fall morning."
~ Innkeeper, Maine Stay Inn & Cottages

1½	cups old-fashioned rolled oats
2	cups milk
⅓	cup vegetable oil
2	large eggs
¾	cup all-purpose flour
2	tablespoons sugar
2½	teaspoons baking powder
1	teaspoon salt
1	teaspoon cinnamon
½	teaspoon allspice
½	teaspoon ground cloves
2	apples, peeled and cut into ¼-inch dice

Maple syrup and/or hot applesauce, for serving

Preheat and lightly grease an electric griddle to 375-390°F or a skillet over medium heat. Put oats in a bowl. Pour milk over oats and let stand for 2 minutes. Mix in oil, eggs, flour, sugar, baking powder and salt. Mix in cinnamon, allspice and cloves. Stir in apples. Cook pancakes until golden brown on both sides. Serve with maple syrup and/or hot applesauce.

Inn at Blush Hill

The Inn at Blush Hill is a Cape Cod-style bed & breakfast built in 1790. The inn was once a stagecoach stopover, and is now known as the oldest inn in Waterbury. Set on five rolling acres, high on a hilltop, it offers unrestricted views of the Green Mountains. Vermont's best ski resorts and most charming towns are only minutes away.

In the kitchen, a large double fireplace serves as a cozy backdrop for a full country breakfasts served at the long, pine farmhands' table. A bay window offers panoramic views of the sunrise during meals.

INNKEEPERS:	Pamela Gosselin
ADDRESS:	784 Blush Hill Road
	Waterbury, Vermont 05676
TELEPHONE:	(802) 244-7529; (800) 736-7522
E-MAIL:	inn@blushhill.com
WEBSITE:	www.blushhill.com
ROOMS:	5 Rooms; Private baths
CHILDREN:	Children age 6 and older welcome
ANIMALS:	Not allowed
HANDICAPPED:	Not handicapped accessible
DIETARY NEEDS:	Will accommodate guests' special dietary needs

Four-Berry Pancakes

Makes 4 Servings

"This recipe was the Blue Ribbon Breakfast Winner in the American Bed & Breakfast Association's Recipe Contest. It was published in the book Innkeepers' Finest Breakfasts *by Jessica Bennet." ~ Innkeeper, Inn at Blush Hill*

1½	cups all-purpose flour
2	tablespoons sugar
1	teaspoon salt
1	teaspoon baking powder
3	tablespoons oil
2	large eggs
½	cup plain yogurt
¾	cup milk
3	cups mixed fresh berries (blueberries, raspberries, strawberries, blackberries, etc.), divided

Ben & Jerry's vanilla ice cream, for serving
Vermont maple syrup, warmed, for serving

In a large bowl, combine flour, sugar, salt and baking powder. In a medium bowl, combine oil, eggs, yogurt and milk. Add egg mixture to flour mixture; mix well. Gently fold 1 cup of berries into batter.

Pour batter by ¼-cupsful onto a hot, oiled griddle or skillet. Cook until golden brown on both sides. Arrange 3 pancakes on each plate. Top each serving with a scoop of ice cream, ½ cup of berries and warm maple syrup.

Bear Mountain Inn

The circa 1915 Bear Mountain Inn offers visitors all of the comforts of home with a stunning backdrop of Maine's natural beauty. Lakeside lodges are available for those who seek a more rustic atmosphere and a little more privacy. Nestled in 52 acres of private country charm, this four-season inn hosts guests in complete tranquility.

Relax on the spacious porch while planning a day of hiking, swimming, fishing, boating or bird watching. Comfortable common rooms offer a place to unwind and mingle, while bedrooms offer rustic luxury.

INNKEEPERS:	Lorraine Blais
ADDRESS:	364 Waterford Road
	Waterford, Maine 04088
TELEPHONE:	(207) 583-4404
E-MAIL:	innkeeper@bearmtninn.com
WEBSITE:	www.bearmtninn.com
ROOMS:	8 Rooms; 2 Suites; 1 Cottage; Private baths
CHILDREN:	Welcome
ANIMALS:	Not allowed; Resident dogs, cats, goats, sheep, etc.
HANDICAPPED:	Not handicapped accessible
DIETARY NEEDS:	Will accommodate guests' special dietary needs

Sour Cream, Peach & Blueberry Pancakes

Makes 6 Servings

"This dish is a cross between a French crêpe and a Maine pancake. It is light and delicious." ~ Innkeeper, Bear Mountain Inn

1	cup sour cream
5	large eggs
1	tablespoon water
½	teaspoon butter extract
1	teaspoon vanilla extract
1	teaspoon baking soda
1	teaspoon baking powder
½	teaspoon salt
¼	cup white sugar
3½	tablespoons packed brown sugar
1	cup unbleached all-purpose flour
½	teaspoon cinnamon

Thinly sliced peeled peaches
Fresh Maine blueberries

Preheat oven to 350°F. In a large bowl, beat sour cream, eggs, water, butter extract and vanilla with a mixer on medium speed for 2 minutes. In a small bowl, combine baking soda, baking powder, salt, white and brown sugar, flour and cinnamon. Slowly mix flour mixture into sour cream mixture.

Pour batter onto a preheated, greased griddle or skillet. Once pancakes begin to bubble, top with a few peach slices and some blueberries. Turn pancakes and cook for 1 minute longer, or until done.

Chimney Crest Manor

Chimney Crest Manor is housed in a splendid Tudor mansion overlooking Connecticut's Farmington Hills. The inn was built in 1930 in what is now the Federal Hill Historic District of Bristol. The inn's ornate plasterwork, beamed ceilings, framed artwork and stately fireplaces express a grandeur unparalleled in the area.

Activities abound within a 30-mile radius of the inn. State parks and many of the state's finest restaurants, vineyards and museums are within a few miles. Antique hunters will be entranced by the dozens of nearby shops.

INNKEEPERS:	Cynthia & Dante Cimadamore
ADDRESS:	5 Founders Drive
	Bristol, Connecticut 06010
TELEPHONE:	(860) 582-4219
E-MAIL:	chimnycrst@aol.com
WEBSITE:	www.bbonline.com/ct/chimneycrest
ROOMS:	2 Rooms; 3 Suites; Private baths
CHILDREN:	Children age 10 and older welcome
ANIMALS:	Not allowed; Resident dog
HANDICAPPED:	Not handicapped accessible
DIETARY NEEDS:	Will accommodate guests' special dietary needs

Yogurt Pancakes

Makes 3 Servings

"Makes a light, tasty pancake your guests will love!" - Innkeeper, Chimney Crest Manor Bed & Breakfast

1½	cups unbleached, all-purpose flour, sifted
1	teaspoon salt
1	teaspoon sugar
1	teaspoon baking powder
½	teaspoon baking soda
1	cup milk
1	(8-ounce) carton flavored yogurt (vanilla is good)

Club soda
Maple syrup, for serving (optional)

Combine flour, salt, sugar, baking powder and baking soda. Add milk and yogurt; mix until batter is smooth. Add club soda, as needed, to lighten batter. Cook pancakes on a preheated, greased griddle or skillet until golden brown on both sides. Serve with maple syrup, if desired.

Adair Country Inn

Flavorful food, made with only the freshest ingredients and artfully presented, is a major focus at Adair County Inn. The intimate dining room has a fireplace and wonderful views of the inn's gardens. The full breakfast includes a buffet of baked granola, yogurt, piping hot popovers, Vermont cob-smoked bacon, maple sausage, house baked breads and a hot entrée made with farm-fresh eggs.

In summer, guests can hike, canoe or play golf or tennis. In winter, the inn is within an hour of several world-class downhill and nordic ski areas.

INNKEEPERS:	Judy & Bill Whitman
ADDRESS:	80 Guider Lane
	Bethlehem, New Hampshire 03574
TELEPHONE:	(603) 444-2600; (888) 444-2600
E-MAIL:	innkeeper@adairinn.com
WEBSITE:	www.adairinn.com
ROOMS:	8 Rooms; 1 Suite; 1 Cottage; Private baths
CHILDREN:	Children age 12 and older welcome
ANIMALS:	Not allowed; Resident cat
HANDICAPPED:	Not handicapped accessible
DIETARY NEEDS:	Will accommodate guests' special dietary needs

Apple Clafouti

Makes 4 to 6 Servings

"This is one of the most popular breakfast offerings at Adair. Why? It's pure comfort food – soft, eggy, sweet and cinnamony. It is wonderful simply served sprinkled with powdered sugar, but keep a jug of real New Hampshire maple syrup nearby!" - Innkeeper, Adair Country Inn

1	cup all-purpose flour
3	tablespoons sugar
¼	teaspoon salt
4	eggs
1	cup heavy cream
1	teaspoon vanilla extract
5	tablespoons butter, melted and divided
2-3	apples, thinly sliced
2	tablespoons brown sugar
½	teaspoon cinnamon

Powdered sugar, for garnish
Maple syrup, for serving

Preheat oven to 350°F. Combine flour, sugar and salt. Whisk in eggs, cream and vanilla. Add 3 tablespoons of melted butter and stir until smooth.

Heat a 9- or 10-inch oven-proof skillet over medium-low heat. Spray skillet with non-stick cooking spray or melt a small amount of butter in skillet. Add batter to skillet and cook until it begins to set

Combine brown sugar and cinnamon. Add apple slices and toss to coat. Layer apple slices in a decorative pattern on batter in skillet. Drizzle remaining 2 tablespoons of melted butter over apples. Put skillet in oven and bake for 15-20 minutes, until center is firm. Slice and serve.

The Birds Nest Inn

Welcome to the Birds Nest Inn, a warm and cozy Vermont bed & breakfast surrounded by stately black locust trees. The inn is centrally located between Stowe and Waterbury, offering a tranquil New England mountain getaway.

The Birds Nest Inn is a member of the Vermont Fresh Network and features Vermont products. All your senses will be tantalized – from savoring a three-course, candlelit breakfast with Ben & Jerry's ice cream, to relaxing in the evening with complimentary wine and hors d'oerves.

INNKEEPERS:	Len, Nancy & Valerie Vignola
ADDRESS:	5088 Waterbury-Stowe Road
	Waterbury Center, Vermont 05677
TELEPHONE:	(802) 244-7490; (800) 366-5592
E-MAIL:	nestlein@birdsnestinn.com
WEBSITE:	www.birdsnestinn.com
ROOMS:	6 Rooms; Private baths
CHILDREN:	Not allowed
ANIMALS:	Not allowed; Resident dogs
HANDICAPPED:	Not handicapped accessible
DIETARY NEEDS:	Will accommodate guests' special dietary needs

Maple-Apple Waffles with Ben & Jerry's Ice Cream

Makes 4 to 6 Servings

Maple apples:
- 2 tablespoons butter (preferably Cabot from Vermont)
- 3 apples, peeled and sliced into thin wedges
- ¼ teaspoon cinnamon
- 2 tablespoons sugar
- ¼ cup pure Vermont maple syrup

Waffles:
- 4 large eggs, separated
- 1 tablespoon sugar
- ½ stick butter, melted and cooled
- 1 cup milk
- 1 teaspoon vanilla extract
- 2 cups all-purpose flour
- 2 teaspoons baking powder

Ben & Jerry's ice cream, for topping
Aerosol whipped cream (preferably Cabot from Vermont), for topping

For the maple apples: Melt butter in a skillet over medium heat. Add apples, cinnamon, sugar and maple syrup; toss to coat. Cook until apples are partially soft, yet still firm. Set aside and keep warm.

For the waffles: In a large bowl, beat egg yolks and sugar until light. Mix in butter, milk and vanilla. Add flour and baking powder; beat well. In a medium bowl, beat egg whites until stiff; gently fold into egg yolk mixture. Bake waffles in a preheated, deep-pocketed waffle iron until cover opens easily and waffles are golden brown. Serve immediately on warm plates, topped with maple apples, a big scoop of ice cream and whipped cream.

Camden Windward House

Camden is often referred to as Maine's prettiest seacoast village. Situated at the heart of beautiful Penobscot Bay, Camden is convenient to all Mid-Coast Maine destinations. The circa 1854 Camden Windward House Bed & Breakfast is located in the historic district, just one block from shops, restaurants and the scenic harbor.

"Great location, guest rooms with all the amenities and an exquisite attention to detail by the innkeepers. All in all, this is the finest B&B we have stayed in during more than 15 years of B&B'ing." ~ Guests, Virginia

INNKEEPERS:	Phil & Liane Brookes
ADDRESS:	6 High Street
	Camden, Maine 04843
TELEPHONE:	(207) 236-9656; (877) 492-9656
E-MAIL:	bnb@windwardhouse.com
WEBSITE:	www.windwardhouse.com
ROOMS:	5 Rooms; 3 Suites; Private baths
CHILDREN:	Children age 12 and older welcome
ANIMALS:	Not allowed; Resident dogs & cat
HANDICAPPED:	Call ahead
DIETARY NEEDS:	Will accommodate guests' special dietary needs

Wicked Good Belgian Waffles with Maine Blueberry Compote

Makes 8 to 10 Waffles

"Belgian waffles were introduced to America at the 1964 World's Fair in New York, while Maine blueberries have been a staple of family meals for generations. The two come together in this recipe." ~ Innkeeper, The Camden Windward House

Belgian waffles:
- 2¼   teaspoons active dry yeast
- 2¾   cups warm milk, divided, plus ¼ cup lukewarm milk
- 3   large eggs, separated
- 1½   sticks unsalted butter, melted and cooled
- ½   cup sugar
- 1½   teaspoons salt
- 2   teaspoons vanilla extract
- 4   cups all-purpose flour

Maine blueberry compote:
- 2   cups fresh Maine blueberries
- ¼   cup pure Maine maple syrup

For the waffles: Whisk together yeast and ¼ cup of warm milk; let stand for about 5 minutes. In a large bowl, whisk together egg yolks, ¼ cup of lukewarm milk and butter. Whisk yeast mixture, sugar, salt and vanilla into egg yolk mixture. Add flour in 3 parts, alternating with remaining 2½ cups of warm milk in 2 parts. In a medium bowl, beat egg whites until soft peaks form; fold into batter. Cover tightly with plastic wrap and let stand in a warm place (such as an unheated oven) for about 1 hour, until doubled in size. Stir down batter. Bake waffles on a preheated waffle iron until golden brown. Serve with warm blueberry compote.

For the blueberry compote: Bring blueberries and maple syrup to a boil in a saucepan. Lower heat and simmer until thickened.

Craignair Inn

Set on a granite ledge rising from the sea and surrounded by flower gardens, Craignair Inn was built in 1928 to house workers from the nearby quarries. The boarding house was converted to an inn in 1940. Little has changed here since the turn of the century – you can still feel the aura of a once lively working town.

The downstairs has a parlor and library, with a sunny dining room looking out on the ocean. Bedrooms are comfortably furnished with quilt-covered beds and antique furniture – most offer breathtaking views of the ocean.

INNKEEPERS:	Steve & Neva Joseph
ADDRESS:	5 Third Street
	Spruce Head, Maine 04859
TELEPHONE:	(207) 594-7644; (800) 320-9997
E-MAIL:	innkeeper@craignair.com
WEBSITE:	www.craignair.com
ROOMS:	20 Rooms; Private & shared baths
CHILDREN:	Welcome
ANIMALS:	Dogs welcome; call ahead
HANDICAPPED:	Not handicapped accessible
DIETARY NEEDS:	Will accommodate guests' special dietary needs

Apple Waffles with Apple Cider Syrup

Makes 4 Servings

3	eggs, separated
1	cup milk
1	stick butter, melted and cooled
½	cup grated apple, plus sliced apples, for garnish
1	cup all-purpose flour
½	cup whole-wheat flour
1	tablespoon baking powder
1	tablespoon sugar
1	teaspoon salt
1	teaspoon nutmeg
½	teaspoon cinnamon

Apple cider syrup:

2	cups apple cider
1	teaspoon nutmeg
½	teaspoon cinnamon
½	cup maple syrup

Beat egg whites to stiff peaks; set aside. In a small bowl, mix egg yolks, milk, butter and apple until well combined. In a large bowl, combine all-purpose and whole-wheat flour, baking powder, sugar, salt, nutmeg and cinnamon. Add egg mixture to flour mixture and stir just until moistened. Gently fold in egg whites. Bake waffles in a preheated waffle iron until golden brown. Serve with apple slices and apple cider syrup.

For the apple cider syrup: Combine cider, nutmeg and cinnamon in a small saucepan. Bring to a boil, lower heat and simmer until reduced by half. Stir in maple syrup and simmer until slightly thickened.

Manor House

Indulge yourself in a romantic retreat at the Manor House Bed & Breakfast, a historic, circa 1898 mansion built for the leisure class of an earlier era. Find yourself surrounded by Victorian elegance as you walk through rooms adorned with Tiffany windows, classic architectural details and antique furnishings.

Guest rooms overlook the spacious grounds and gardens. Rooms are furnished with period antiques and luxurious down comforters. Several offer fireplaces, private balconies and oversized Jacuzzi or soaking tubs.

INNKEEPERS:	Diane & Henry Tremblay
ADDRESS:	69 Maple Avenue
	Norfolk, Connecticut 06058
TELEPHONE:	(860) 542-5690
E-MAIL:	innkeeper@manorhouse-norfolk.com
WEBSITE:	www.manorhouse-norfolk.com
ROOMS:	8 Rooms; 1 Suite; Private baths
CHILDREN:	Children age 12 and older welcome
ANIMALS:	Not allowed
HANDICAPPED:	Not handicapped accessible
DIETARY NEEDS:	Will accommodate guests' special dietary needs

Orange Waffles

Makes 8 Servings

1	cup all-purpose flour
1	tablespoon sugar
¼	teaspoon salt
1½	teaspoons baking powder
⅛	teaspoon nutmeg
2	eggs
½	cup milk

Grated zest of 1 orange
2 tablespoons butter, melted
Powdered sugar, for garnish

Preheat oven to 350°F. Combine flour, sugar, salt, baking powder, nutmeg, eggs, milk and orange zest; beat until smooth. Add butter and stir until combined. Bake waffles until golden brown. Sprinkle with powdered sugar to serve.

Tip: These waffles are delicious with fruit syrup, such as cherry syrup, or serve with them whipped cream or chantilly cream mixed with a little grated orange zest for a "Creamsicle" waffle.

French Toast, Bread Puddings & Crêpes

Apple Ginger Upside-Down French Toast 99

Banana Bread French Toast..101

Frangelico-Nutella French Toast 103

Blackberry-Stuffed French Toast 105

Strawberry Banana French Toast..107

Raisin Pecan French Toast 109

Blueberry Morning Glory..111

Caramelized Apple Bread Pudding 113

Cranberry Bread Pudding..115

Pumpkin Bread Pudding 117

Apple Raisin Bread Pudding...119

Apple Crêpes 121

French Banana Crêpes 123

Memère's French Crêpes...125

French Toast, Bread Puddings & Crêpes

Birchwood Inn

The Birchwood Inn Bed & Breakfast has been welcoming guests with warmth and hospitality since 1767. Antiques, collectibles, featherbeds, quilts and down comforters are very much at home in this Colonial Revival bed & breakfast mansion, the only Lenox inn listed on the National Register of Historic Places.

Secluded among white birches, stately oaks and towering pines, the inn has the pastoral stillness of a country morning yet is only a short walk from the celebrated restaurants, shops and galleries of historic Lenox village.

INNKEEPERS:	Ellen Gutman Chenaux
ADDRESS:	7 Hubbard Street
	Lenox, Massachusetts 01240
TELEPHONE:	(413) 637-2600; (800) 524-1646
E-MAIL:	innkeeper@birchwood-inn.com
WEBSITE:	www.birchwood-inn.com
ROOMS:	10 Rooms; 1 Suite; Private baths
CHILDREN:	Children age 12 and older welcome
ANIMALS:	Not allowed; Resident dog
HANDICAPPED:	Not handicapped accessible
DIETARY NEEDS:	Will accommodate guests' special dietary needs

Apple Ginger Upside-Down French Toast

This French toast is best prepared the night before and baked in the morning.

Makes 8 Servings

1	stick butter
2	tablespoons water
1	cup packed brown sugar
2	cups sliced peeled apples
8-10	slices challah or brioche bread
½	cup finely chopped candied ginger
5	large eggs
1½	cups milk
2	teaspoons vanilla extract
1	teaspoon ground ginger

Cinnamon, to taste

Preheat oven to 350°F. Grease a 9x13-inch baking pan. Melt butter in a small saucepan over low heat. Add brown sugar and water; stir until smooth. Pour butter mixture into baking pan. Arrange apple slices on top of butter mixture. Sprinkle candied ginger over apples. Layer bread slices on top of ginger.

Beat together eggs, milk, vanilla, ground ginger and cinnamon; pour evenly over bread (if time allows, cover and refrigerate overnight). Bake for 45-55 minutes. Cut French toast into 8 pieces and invert onto serving plates. Drizzle some pan syrup over each serving.

Note: In summer, you can substitute peaches or plums for the apples.

One Centre Street Inn

The circa 1824, Antique Greek Revival One Centre Street Inn is set amongst stately sea captains' homes and parsonages. The inn is centrally located on Olde Kings Highway (Route 6A), the most beautiful and scenic travel route on all of Cape Cod, and is a short walk or bike ride to wonderful vintage bookstores, antique shops, fine restaurants, art galleries, great golf courses and Gray's Beach.

Guest rooms are uniquely decorated in historic colors and are named for prominent people who lived in Yarmouth Port around the 1800s.

INNKEEPERS:	Carla Masse
ADDRESS:	One Centre Street
	Yarmouth Port, Massachusetts 02675
TELEPHONE:	(508) 362-9951; (866) 362-9951
E-MAIL:	sales@onecentrestreetinn.com
WEBSITE:	www.onecentrestreetinn.com
ROOMS:	4 Rooms; 1 Suite; Private & shared baths
CHILDREN:	Children age 12 and older welcome
ANIMALS:	Not allowed; Resident dog
HANDICAPPED:	Not handicapped accessible
DIETARY NEEDS:	Will accommodate guests' special dietary needs

Banana Bread French Toast

Makes 4 Servings

"What a nice alternative to plain French toast!" - Innkeeper, One Center Street Inn

Grated zest and juice of 1 orange
1 large orange
3 large eggs
¾ cup milk
½ teaspoon cinnamon
⅛ teaspoon nutmeg
2 tablespoons sugar
1½ teaspoons vanilla extract
8 slices banana bread (see recipe on page 15)
Butter or margarine

Rum sauce:
2 tablespoons butter or margarine
2 tablespoons brown sugar
2 bananas, sliced into 1-inch-thick slices
1 teaspoon rum flavoring or rum, or to taste
2 cups maple syrup

Combine orange zest, orange juice, eggs, milk, cinnamon, nutmeg, sugar and vanilla; whisk until sugar dissolves.

Melt butter or margarine on a griddle or skillet over medium heat. Dip banana bread in egg mixture, turning to coat both sides. Cook banana bread for 2-3 minutes per side. Serve with warm rum sauce.

For the rum sauce: Combine butter, brown sugar and bananas in a saucepan over medium heat; stir gently until sugar dissolves. Add maple syrup and stir to combine.

Mt. Washington

Surrounded by the White Mountains, the Mt. Washington Bed & Breakfast is located on five acres in the Androscoggin River Valley. The inn sits on a hill overlooking Reflection Pond, which is fed by the Androscoggin River. To the south is the Presidential Range and Mount Washington. Hike, bike, canoe, ski, shop or just relax on the porch.

Rooms are named after birds in the area. Each is individually decorated with handmade quilts, antique furniture, fluffy robes, scented glycerin soaps and bath and shower scents.

INNKEEPERS:	Mary Ann Mayer
ADDRESS:	421 State Route 2
	Shelburne, New Hampshire 03581
TELEPHONE:	(603) 466-2669; (877) 466-2399
E-MAIL:	mtwashbb@yahoo.com
WEBSITE:	www.mtwashingtonbb.com
ROOMS:	7 Rooms; Private baths
CHILDREN:	Children age 12 and older welcome
ANIMALS:	Not allowed
HANDICAPPED:	Not handicapped accessible
DIETARY NEEDS:	Will accommodate guests' special dietary needs

Frangelico-Nutella French Toast

Makes 8 Servings

"A wonderful Valentine's Day breakfast for your special someone." – Innkeeper, Mt. Washington Bed & Breakfast

8	large eggs
½	cup half & half
1	shot (¼ cup) Frangelico or other hazelnut liqueur
2	loaves Italian bread, sliced ½- to 1-inch thick

Nutella, to taste*
Powdered sugar, for garnish
Sliced fresh strawberries, for garnish
Maple syrup, for serving

Whisk together eggs, half & half and Frangelico until well blended. Dip bread in egg mixture, turning to coat. Cook on a lightly greased, preheated griddle or skillet until browned on both sides. Spread Nutella on 1 side of each piece of French toast (thickly or thinly, to your taste). Sprinkle very lightly with powdered sugar. Garnish with sliced strawberries. Serve with warm maple syrup, if desired.

*Note: Nutella is a chocolate and hazelnut spread. It is available in the peanut butter section of larger groceries.

Wildflower Inn

Tucked into the rolling hills of the Northeast Kingdom of Vermont, the Wildflower Inn is a 570-acre Vermont country resort. The inn offers hiking and mountain biking, cross-country skiing, downhill skiing at Burke Mountain Resort, snowshoeing, snowmobiling, horse-drawn wagon and sleigh rides, extensive flower gardens and a petting barn.

"This grand inn high on a 1,000-foot ridge welcomes your family with warm hospitality and tons of kids' activities. The dining room is notable for its eclectic cuisine. The scenery and recreation are top-notch" ~ *Yankee Magazine*

INNKEEPERS:	Jim & Mary O'Reilly
ADDRESS:	2059 Darling Hill Road
	Lyndonville, Vermont 05851
TELEPHONE:	(802) 626-8310; (800) 627-8310
E-MAIL:	info@wildflowerinn.com
WEBSITE:	www.wildflowerinn.com
ROOMS:	10 Rooms; 14 Suites; Private baths
CHILDREN:	Children welcome
ANIMALS:	Not allowed
HANDICAPPED:	Handicapped accessible
DIETARY NEEDS:	Will accommodate guests' special dietary needs

Blackberry-Stuffed French Toast

Makes 6 Servings

"This recipe can be adapted to use any seasonal berries." ~ Innkeeper, Wildflower Inn

2	(8-ounce) packages cream cheese, softened
1	cup blackberries
½	cup honey, warmed slightly (aids mixing)

Pinch of nutmeg

6	large eggs
½	cup heavy cream
1	tablespoon vanilla extract
1	tablespoon cinnamon
1	loaf homemade bread, sliced

Cinnamon-sugar, for garnish
Vermont maple syrup, for serving

Stir together cream cheese, blackberries, honey and nutmeg just until loosely blended. Spread cream cheese mixture on one side of ½ of bread slices. Sandwich with remaining bread slices.

Beat together eggs, cream, vanilla and cinnamon. Dip sandwiches into egg mixture, turning to coat both sides. Cook on a buttered griddle or skillet until golden brown on both sides. Dust with cinnamon-sugar and serve with warm maple syrup.

I.B. Munson House

Experience the enchantment of a bygone era at this Vermont Victorian inn. From the first step you take into the I.B. Munson House, you cannot help but be swept back in time. A beautiful chandelier lights the way as a gently curving staircase leads you to your room.

You'll feel like royalty amidst the 12-foot ceilings and period architectural details, including arched windows and elaborate moldings. Rock on the front porch and watch the town go about its business or relax on the more secluded side porch and gaze at the gardens.

INNKEEPERS:	Lisa & Charlie McClafferty
ADDRESS:	37 South Main Street
	Wallingford, Vermont 05773
TELEPHONE:	(802) 446-2860; (888) 519-3771
E-MAIL:	stay@ibmunsoninn.com
WEBSITE:	www.ibmunsoninn.com
ROOMS:	7 Rooms; Private baths
CHILDREN:	Children age 12 and older welcome
ANIMALS:	Not allowed; Resident dog
HANDICAPPED	Not handicapped accessible
DIETARY NEEDS:	Will accommodate guests' special dietary needs

Strawberry Banana French Toast

Makes 12 Servings

"This French toast looks and tastes great. Plan ahead – it needs to be started the night before." – Innkeeper, I.B. Munson House B&B

1	loaf French bread, cut into ½-inch-thick slices
5	large eggs
¾	cup milk
¼	teaspoon baking powder
1	tablespoon vanilla extract
1	(20-ounce) package frozen whole strawberries
4	ripe bananas, sliced
1	cup sugar
1	tablespoon apple pie spice (or a mixture of cinnamon, nutmeg and allspice
2	tablespoons cinnamon-sugar

Powdered sugar, for garnish

Put bread in a 9x13-inch baking dish. Combine eggs, milk, baking powder and vanilla; pour over bread. Cover and refrigerate overnight.

The next day, preheat oven to 450°F. Combine strawberries, bananas, sugar and apple pie spice; place in a greased 9x13-inch baking pan. Top with bread mixture. Sprinkle with cinnamon-sugar. Bake for 20-25 minutes. Put 2 slices of French toast on each plate. Spoon fruit and pan juices over each serving. Sprinkle with powdered sugar to serve.

The Inn at Rutland

The Inn at Rutland is a stately, circa 1889 Victorian Mansion located within a few miles of Killington. This Vermont inn is a perfect place to stay for people skiing at Killington, hiking the Green Mountains or enjoying the fall foliage. Fronted by a large wraparound porch, the inn affords breathtaking views of the Green Mountains.

Inside the inn, the grand oak staircase, carved plaster relief ceilings and wainscoting, leaded glass windows and fine antiques take you back to an era of 19th century romantic splendor.

INNKEEPERS:	Leslie & Steven Brenner
ADDRESS:	70 North Main Street
	Rutland, Vermont 05701
TELEPHONE:	(802) 773-0575; (800) 808-0575
E-MAIL:	stay@innatrutland.com
WEBSITE:	www.innatrutland.com
ROOMS:	11 Rooms; Private baths
CHILDREN:	Welcome
ANIMALS:	Not allowed
HANDICAPPED:	Not handicapped accessible
DIETARY NEEDS:	Will accommodate guests' special dietary needs

Raisin Pecan French Toast

Makes 6 Servings

Plan ahead – this French toast needs to be started the night before.

- 6   large eggs
- 1¼   cups milk
- 1   teaspoon vanilla extract
- ¼   teaspoon nutmeg
- ¼   teaspoon cinnamon
- 6   slices cinnamon raisin bread

Topping:
- ½   stick butter, softened
- ⅓   cup chopped pecans
- ½   cup packed dark brown sugar
- 1   tablespoon light corn syrup

Powdered sugar, for garnish
Orange slices, for garnish

Whisk together eggs, milk, vanilla, nutmeg and cinnamon. Place bread in a single layer in a buttered 9x13-inch baking dish. Pour egg mixture over bread. Cover and refrigerate overnight.

The next day, preheat oven to 350°F. Uncover French toast and carefully spread topping over bread. Bake for 45 minutes. Serve on plates lightly dusted with cinnamon. Sprinkle powdered sugar over each serving and, if desired, over plate. Garnish with orange slices to serve.

For the topping: Combine all topping ingredients.

Brook Farm Inn

Located just down the hill and around the bend from the center of historic Lenox, Brook Farm Inn welcomes guests to the grace of its Victorian past and the comforts of the present. Tastefully furnished, this 130-year-old home offers comfort and tranquility surrounded by the beauty of the Berkshires and a tradition of poetry and literature.

Start your day with a sumptuous breakfast. Then take the short walk into town, where you can find charming boutiques, discover antique treasures, view fine art in many galleries and dine in splendid restaurants.

INNKEEPERS:	Linda & Phil Halpern
ADDRESS:	15 Hawthorne Street
	Lenox, Massachusetts 01240
TELEPHONE:	(413) 637-3013; (800) 285-7638
E-MAIL:	innkeeper@brookfarm.com
WEBSITE:	www.brookfarm.com
ROOMS:	14 Rooms; 1 Suite; Private baths
CHILDREN:	Infants and children age 15 and older welcome
ANIMALS:	Not allowed
HANDICAPPED:	Handicapped accessible
DIETARY NEEDS:	Will accommodate guests' special dietary needs

Blueberry Morning Glory

Makes 12 Servings

"This rich casserole can be made with fresh or frozen blueberries. It's spectacular served with hot blueberry sauce. It can be prepared ahead of time, covered and refrigerated." - Innkeeper, Brook Farm Inn

1	loaf Challah bread or unsliced white bread, crusts removed
1	(8-ounce) package cream cheese, cut into small pieces
2	cups fresh or frozen blueberries
8	large eggs
⅓	cup maple syrup
½	cup sugar
2	cups half & half

Blueberry sauce:

1	cup sugar
1	cup water
2	tablespoons cornstarch
1	cup fresh or frozen blueberries

Preheat oven to 350°F. Spray a 9x13-inch glass baking dish with non-stick cooking spray. Tear bread into small pieces and arrange ½ of bread over bottom of baking dish. Scatter cream cheese over bread. Scatter blueberries over cream cheese. Arrange remaining bread on top.

Beat eggs. Add maple syrup, sugar and half & half; mix well. Pour egg mixture evenly over bread (at this point, you can cover and refrigerate overnight). Bake for 50 minutes. Serve with warm blueberry sauce.

For the blueberry sauce: Combine sugar, water and cornstarch in a saucepan over medium heat. Cook for about 5 minutes, stirring constantly, until thickened. Add blueberries and simmer for 10 minutes, stirring occasionally.

The Inn & Vineyard at Chester

The Inn & Vineyard at Chester is a sanctuary amid the natural beauty of the Connecticut River Valley. The inn is set among rolling hills near the Connecticut Wine Trail, one of America's most popular destinations. Chester is a picture-perfect New England town. It is renowned for its fine restaurants, antique shops, art galleries, the Norma Terris Theater and the internationally acclaimed, Tony Award-winning Goodspeed Opera House.

The newly decorated and renovated rooms and suites feature pencil-post beds with orthopedic mattresses and beautiful antique furnishings.

INNKEEPERS:	Edward J. Safdie
ADDRESS:	318 West Main Street
	Chester, Connecticut 06412
TELEPHONE:	(860) 526-9541
E-MAIL:	info@innatchester.com
WEBSITE:	www.innatchester.com
ROOMS:	44 Rooms; 4 Suites; 1 Cottage; Private baths
CHILDREN:	Children age 12 and older welcome
ANIMALS:	Not allowed
HANDICAPPED:	Handicapped accessible
DIETARY NEEDS:	Will accommodate guests' special dietary needs

Caramelized Apple Bread Pudding

Makes 6 to 8 Servings

"As part of our November Apple Fest, chef Michael Fichtel developed this amazing bread pudding. Two- or three-day-old bread makes the perfect bread pudding. If your bread is fresh, simply let it sit out uncovered for an hour." - Innkeeper, Inn & Vineyard at Chester

- ½ stick unsalted butter
- 1 cup sugar, divided
- 4 apples, peeled and cut into ¼-inch-thick slices
- 2 cups whole milk
- 5 large eggs
- ⅔ teaspoon cinnamon
- ½ loaf white bread (crusts removed), sliced into 1-inch cubes (about 7-8 slices)

Whipped cream, for serving
Cinnamon-sugar, for garnish

Combine butter, ½ cup of sugar and apples in a large skillet over medium-high heat. Cook for 15 minutes, stirring frequently, until apples are nicely caramelized. Remove apples and cool for 10-15 minutes.

In a bowl, whisk together remaining ½ cup of sugar, milk, eggs and cinnamon. Gently fold bread and apples into egg mixture. Transfer to a buttered 8x8-inch glass baking dish. Cover and refrigerate for 2 hours.

Preheat oven to 350°F. Bake bread pudding for 45-55 minutes. (The bread pudding will puff up and brown as it bakes. As it cools, it will settle slightly.) Serve warm or at room temperature, topped with whipped cream and a sprinkling of cinnamon-sugar.

The Inn at Ormsby Hill

Renowned for comfort, heartfelt hospitality and profound attention to detail, the Inn at Ormsby Hill is an ideal retreat where guests are totally pampered with exquisite accommodations, excellent food and unparalleled amenities. Whether you come for relaxation, romance or recreation, the Inn at Ormsby Hill will make your Vermont getaway an unforgettable event.

Imagine stylish decor of the highest quality – a canopy bed, a private Jacuzzi for two, a glowing fireplace. It is a potion for romance. Room design and ambience was created with tranquility and comfort as the guiding principles.

INNKEEPERS:	Ted & Chris Sprague
ADDRESS:	1842 Main Street
	Manchester Center, Vermont 05255
TELEPHONE:	(802) 362-1163; (800) 670-2841
E-MAIL:	stay@ormsbyhill.com
WEBSITE:	www.ormsbyhill.com
ROOMS:	10 Rooms; Private baths
CHILDREN:	Children age 14 and older welcome
ANIMALS:	Not allowed; Resident dog
HANDICAPPED:	Handicapped accessible
DIETARY NEEDS:	Will accommodate guests' special dietary needs

Cranberry Bread Pudding

Makes 10 to 12 Servings

"This recipe was created for a Thanksgiving article about the Inn at Ormsby Hill in Colonial Homes *magazine. Plan ahead – this dish needs to be started the night before serving." ~ Innkeeper, The Inn at Ormsby Hill*

4	cups water
4½	cups sugar, divided
3	tablespoons grated lemon zest
1	vanilla bean, split lengthwise
2	pounds cranberries
2	(1-pound) loaves challah bread, cut into 1-inch cubes
4	teaspoons cinnamon, divided
2	sticks butter, melted
5	cups heavy cream
5	cups milk
18	large eggs

Preheat oven to 350°F. In a large saucepan, bring water, 2 cups of sugar, vanilla bean and lemon zest to a boil; stir to dissolve sugar. Add cranberries; simmer for 1 minute. Remove from heat. Scrape vanilla bean seeds into cranberry mixture; discard vanilla bean pod. Cool to room temperature. Put bread in a large bowl. Add 4 tablespoons of sugar, 2 teaspoons of cinnamon and butter; toss to combine. Transfer bread to a baking sheet and bake for 24 minutes.

Combine 4 tablespoons of sugar and 2 teaspoons of cinnamon; sprinkle into a well-greased 10-cup Bundt pan, coating bottom and sides. Put bread mixture in baking dish. Drain cranberry mixture; spread over bread. Whisk together cream, milk, eggs and remaining 2 cups of sugar; pour over bread. Cover and refrigerate overnight.

The next day, preheat oven to 350°F. Cover baking dish with foil. Set baking dish in a larger pan. Add enough hot water to come halfway up sides of baking dish. Bake for 1 hour, or until center is barely set. Remove baking dish from pan and let stand for 5 minutes. Sprinkle with powdered sugar. Slice and serve with breakfast meat of choice.

Belfast Bay Meadows Inn

The Belfast Bay Meadows Inn is situated on five lush acres, overlooking Penobscot Bay. Stunning views are dotted with islands and filled with schooners, pleasure boats and working lobstermen. Watch the white-sailed schooners glide by on the bay or stroll across flowered meadows. The inn is centrally located on the Maine coast, close to Acadia National Park, Bar Harbor, Rockland and Camden.

The inn's signature breakfast dish is a delicious medley of tender lobster, creamy eggs and sweet red bell peppers folded into a delightful omelet.

INNKEEPERS:	Karin Kane
ADDRESS:	192 Northport Avenue
	Belfast, Maine 04915
TELEPHONE:	(207) 338-5715; (800) 335-2370
E-MAIL:	bbmi@baymeadowsinn.com
WEBSITE:	www.baymeadowsinn.com
ROOMS:	19 Rooms; Private baths
CHILDREN:	Welcome
ANIMALS:	Dogs & cats welcome
HANDICAPPED:	Handicapped accessible
DIETARY NEEDS:	Will accommodate guests' special dietary needs

Pumpkin Bread Pudding

Makes 10 to 12 Servings

"A tasty fall or winter dish." ~ Innkeeper, Belfast Bay Meadows Inn

Unsalted butter, softened
¼   cup plus 2 tablespoons brown sugar
1   cup golden raisins
⅓   cup hot water
1   (15-ounce) can pumpkin
4   large eggs
1   cup white sugar
1½ cups milk
2   teaspoons vanilla extract
1   teaspoon ground ginger
1   teaspoon cinnamon
Pinch of salt
1   (12-ounce) loaf day-old bread (whole wheat, white, French, etc.), cut into 1-inch cubes

Preheat oven to 350°F. Butter a 9x9-inch baking dish with unsalted butter. Sprinkle with brown sugar; set aside on a baking sheet. Put raisins in a small bowl and cover with hot water; set aside to plump.

Whisk together pumpkin, eggs, sugar, milk, vanilla, ginger, cinnamon and salt. Add bread and stir until bread has absorbed pumpkin mixture. Drain raisins and stir into pumpkin mixture. Pour pudding into baking dish; smooth top. Bake for about 40 minutes, until center of pudding is set (check after 30 minutes and cover with foil if top is browning too quickly).

1802 House

Ideally located in a tranquil residential neighborhood, the 1802 House is nestled along the 15th fairway of the Cape Arundel golf course. Graced by historic clapboard homes, yet secluded among towering pines and lush private gardens, the inn offers the pastoral stillness of a country morning and the romance of a luminous, star-filled night.

Breakfast, served in the sunny and cheerful dining room, brings unexpected pleasures from "farmhouse fresh" to gourmet, prepared by the innkeepers and served with a spoonful of lively conversation.

INNKEEPERS:	Edric & Mary Ellen Mason
ADDRESS:	15 Locke Street
	Kennebunkport, Maine 04046
TELEPHONE:	(207) 967-5632; (800) 932-5632
E-MAIL:	inquiry@1802inn.com
WEBSITE:	www.1802inn.com
ROOMS:	6 Rooms; 1 Suite; Private baths
CHILDREN:	Children age 12 and older welcome
ANIMALS:	Not allowed
HANDICAPPED:	Not handicapped accessible
DIETARY NEEDS:	Will accommodate guests' special dietary needs

Apple Raisin Bread Pudding

Makes 6 Servings

"Minus the ice cream, this delicate pudding makes a wonderfully indulgent breakfast." - Innkeeper, 1802 House Bed & Breakfast

2	cups whole milk
1	cup sugar
4	large eggs
3	tablespoons unsalted butter, melted
¼	teaspoon cinnamon, plus extra for topping
⅛	teaspoon salt
7	slices white bread (crusts removed), cut into ¾-inch cubes
1	large Granny Smith apple, peeled and cut into ½-inch cubes
⅔	cup raisins

Vanilla ice cream, for serving

Preheat oven to 350°F. Whisk together milk, sugar, eggs, butter, cinnamon and salt. Fold in bread, apples and raisins. Pour bread mixture into a buttered 7x11-inch or 8x8-inch glass baking dish. Bake for 30 minutes. Sprinkle with cinnamon and bake for about 35 minutes longer, until top of pudding is golden and center is set. Spoon pudding into bowls. Top with vanilla ice cream to serve.

Brass Lantern Inn

The Brass Lantern Inn Bed & Breakfast is located on the edge of Stowe. From the cozy fireplaces and soothing whirlpool tubs to the handmade quilts and spectacular mountain views, this charming and authentic Vermont inn defines romance. Exquisite cuisine, glorious shopping and outdoor recreation are just a short walk or drive from your doorstep.

Rooms are decorated in period decor with antique furnishings, wide plank floors, handcrafted quilts and stenciling. Some rooms feature mountain views, canopy beds, whirlpool tubs and gas parlor fireplaces.

INNKEEPERS:	Andy Aldrich
ADDRESS:	717 Maple Street
	Stowe, Vermont 05672
TELEPHONE:	(802) 253-2229; (800) 729-2980
E-MAIL:	info@brasslanterninn.com
WEBSITE:	www.brasslanterninn.com
ROOMS:	9 Rooms; Private baths
CHILDREN:	Call ahead
ANIMALS:	Not allowed
HANDICAPPED:	Not handicapped accessible
DIETARY NEEDS:	Call ahead

Apple Crêpes

Makes 6 Servings

"The apple crêpes were particularly outstanding." ~ The Discerning Traveler

Crêpes:
- 2 large eggs
- 1½ cups milk
- ½ teaspoon salt
- 1 cup all-purpose flour
- 2 tablespoons butter, melted

Filling:
- 3 tablespoons butter
- ⅔ cup packed brown sugar
- ¼ cup raisins
- Grated zest of 1 orange
- 4½ Granny Smith apples, peeled and cut into ¼-inch-thick slices
- 2 tablespoons pure Vermont maple syrup
- 1 teaspoon cornstarch

For the crêpes: Blend all crêpe ingredients in a blender until smooth. Let batter stand for 30 minutes (this will yield more tender crêpes). Lightly coat a crêpe pan or skillet with vegetable oil and heat over medium-high heat. Pour about 3 tablespoons of batter into pan. Rotate pan to coat evenly with batter. Cook crêpe until golden brown, turn and cook other side briefly. Stack crêpes on a plate with waxed paper between crêpes.

For the filling: Melt butter in a skillet over medium heat. Add brown sugar, raisins and orange zest; simmer until sugar is dissolved. Add apples and simmer gently for about 20 minutes. Remove apples. Pour pan syrup into a small saucepan. Return apples to skillet and keep warm. Whisk cornstarch into pan syrup until smooth. Simmer over low heat until reduced to desired consistency. Fill crêpes with apples. Drizzle some pan syrup over crêpes.

Pryor House

The Pryor House is a lovely, circa 1820, Federal-style home overlooking the Kennebec River in Bath, the historic "City of Ships." Located just a few blocks from the heart of town, this classic New England home features an elegant double staircase, wide pine floors and original fireplaces. Its comfortable atmosphere invites guests to escape from everyday life.

Guests can choose from three distinctive rooms, each with a private bath. The Captain's Room boasts a king-size, four-poster bed, decorative fireplace and a window seat overlooking the river.

INNKEEPERS:	Don & Gwenda Pryor
ADDRESS:	360 Front Street
	Bath, Maine 04530
TELEPHONE:	(207) 443-1146
E-MAIL:	pryorhse@suscommaine.com
WEBSITE:	home.gwi.net/~pryorhse (no 'www')
ROOMS:	3 Rooms; Private baths
CHILDREN:	Children age 12 and older welcome
ANIMALS:	Not allowed
HANDICAPPED:	Not handicapped accessible
DIETARY NEEDS:	Will accommodate guests' special dietary needs

French Banana Crêpes

Makes 5 to 6 Servings

Crêpes:
- 1 cup all-purpose flour
- ¼ cup powdered sugar
- 1 cup milk
- 2 eggs
- 3 tablespoons butter or margarine, melted
- 1 teaspoon vanilla extract
- ¼ teaspoon salt

Filling:
- ½ stick butter or margarine
- ¼ cup packed brown sugar
- ¼ teaspoon cinnamon, plus extra for garnish
- ¼ teaspoon nutmeg
- ¼ cup light cream
- 5-6 firm bananas, halved lengthwise
- Whipped cream, for serving (optional)

For the crêpes: Sift together flour and powdered sugar into a bowl. Add milk, eggs, butter, vanilla and salt; beat until smooth. Let batter stand for 30 minutes (this yields more tender crêpes). Heat a lightly greased 6-inch skillet over medium heat. Add about 3 tablespoons of batter; rotate pan so batter covers bottom of skillet. Cook until lightly browned; turn and lightly brown other side. Stack crêpes between sheets of waxed paper on a wire rack. Repeat with remaining batter (makes 10-12 crêpes).

For the filling: Melt together butter, brown sugar, cinnamon and nutmeg in a saucepan over low heat. Stir in cream and cook until slightly thickened. Add ½ of halved bananas; cook for 2-3 minutes, spooning sauce over them. Remove bananas; set aside and keep warm. Repeat with remaining bananas.

To serve: Roll a crêpe around each banana half. Place crêpes on a serving platter. Spoon pan sauce over crêpes. Top with whipped cream and sprinkle with cinnamon.

Ferry Point House

Situated on Lake Winnisquam, the Ferry Point House is a gracious Victorian home built in the early 1800s by the Pillsbury family as a summer retreat. This is a truly picturesque location where you can enjoy romantic moments in the gazebo on the water's edge or join fellow guests on the 60-foot-long veranda overlooking the lake.

The Ferry Point House has seven tastefully decorated guest rooms, all with private baths. The inn's decor and antique furnishing speak of a bygone era while creating an atmosphere of warmth and comfort.

INNKEEPERS:	Diane & Joe Damato
ADDRESS:	100 Lower Bay Road
	Sanbornton, New Hampshire 03269
TELEPHONE:	(603) 524-0087
E-MAIL:	info@ferrypointhouse.com
WEBSITE:	www.ferrypointhouse.com
ROOMS:	9 Rooms; Private baths
CHILDREN:	Children age 10 and older welcome
ANIMALS:	Not allowed; Resident cat (not in public areas)
HANDICAPPED:	Not handicapped accessible
DIETARY NEEDS:	Will accommodate guests' special dietary needs

Memère's French Crêpes

Makes 10 Crêpes

"This is a very special recipe that has been in my family for generations. My grandmother taught my mother and my mother still teaches me. It has taken me about 20 years to learn the proper technique for cooking my grandmother's crêpes. When done to perfection, these crêpes should be thin, crisp and melt in your mouth." ~ Innkeeper, Ferry Point House on Lake Winnisquam

2	cups all-purpose flour
1	teaspoon baking soda
½	teaspoon salt
3	eggs
1¾	cups milk

Solid shortening
Fresh strawberry slices or raspberries, for garnish
Warm maple syrup, for serving

In a medium bowl, combine flour, baking soda and salt. In a small bowl, beat eggs and milk with a whisk; stir into flour mixture until smooth and no lumps remain.

Melt 1 tablespoon of shortening in a cast-iron crêpe pan or skillet over medium-high heat. When shortening begins to smoke, carefully place 2 serving spoonsful of batter in pan in a circular direction. Using back of spoon, quickly spread batter to cover bottom of pan and fill any holes. Turn crêpe when underside browns and sides begin to curl. Brown other side slightly. Repeat with remaining batter. Serve immediately garnished with strawberries or raspberries and topped with warm maple syrup.

Egg Dishes & Breakfast Entrées

Crabby Brie Soufflés 129

Egg Blossoms 131

Baked Eggs in Maple Toast Cups 133

Cornish Baked Eggs 135

Herb-Baked Eggs 137

Savory Smoked Atlantic Salmon Clafoutti 139

Smoked Salmon & Artichoke Frittata 141

Goat Cheese, Asparagus & Spring Onion Frittata 143

Lobster Quiche...145

Crab Quiche...147

Pryor House Sausage Quiche 149

Potato Pancakes with Poached Eggs & Cheddar........................151

Lobster Breakfast Treat 153

Ham & Potato Pie 155

Vermont Cheddar Pie..157

Nantucket Pie...159

Egg Dishes & Breakfast Entrées

1802 House

Come fall under the spell of one of Kennebunkport's most historic and charming bed & breakfast inns. Built in 1802, this beautifully restored farmhouse reflects the relaxed style of a Maine seaside resort and offers elegantly comfortable lodging with all the amenities of a fine country inn.

The Sebago Room is the most luxurious of rooms, located in a private wing of the inn. The bedroom has a four poster canopy bed draped with white organza. The bathroom has a large, marble shower with dual showerheads and a heated tile floor. A separate sitting room has a gas fireplace.

INNKEEPERS:	Edric & Mary Ellen Mason
ADDRESS:	15 Locke Street
	Kennebunkport, Maine 04046
TELEPHONE:	(207) 967-5632; (800) 932-5632
E-MAIL:	inquiry@1802inn.com
WEBSITE:	www.1802inn.com
ROOMS:	6 Rooms; 1 Suite; Private baths
CHILDREN:	Children age 12 and older welcome
ANIMALS:	Not allowed
HANDICAPPED:	Not handicapped accessible
DIETARY NEEDS:	Will accommodate guests' special dietary needs

Crabby Brie Soufflés

Makes 6 Servings

Soufflé:
- ½ stick butter, divided
- 2 tablespoons chopped onion
- 1 cup Maine crabmeat
- ¼ pound Brie cheese, sliced
- ¼ cup all-purpose flour
- 1¼ cups milk, warmed
- 4 egg yolks
- 6 egg whites

Chive sauce:
- ½ cup whipping cream
- ½ cup sour cream
- Juice of ½ lemon
- 5 tablespoons snipped fresh chives

For the soufflé: Preheat oven to 350°F. Butter 6 individual soufflé dishes. Fold each of 6 sheets of foil into thirds. Butter 1 side of each piece of foil and wrap around soufflé dish, buttered-side-in, to form a collar extending 1-inch beyond height of rim. Melt 2 tablespoons of butter in a skillet over medium heat. Add onions and cook until translucent. Add crabmeat and cook until warmed through. Lay slices of Brie on top of crabmeat mixture; cover skillet and cook until cheese is melted.

Melt remaining 2 tablespoons of butter in a small saucepan over medium-low heat. Add flour and cook, stirring, for 4-5 minutes. Slowly add milk and cook, whisking constantly, for 8-10 minutes, until thickened. Whisk in egg yolks. Cook, whisking, for 2 minutes, then pour milk mixture into a bowl. Beat egg whites until stiff, but not dry. Fold crabmeat mixture into milk mixture. Fold in egg whites. Divide mixture among soufflé dishes. Bake for 20-25 minutes. Serve immediately with chive sauce.

For the chive sauce: Mix all sauce ingredients together.

The Arbor Inn

The Arbor Inn is a charming bed & breakfast located on a picturesque road in Rye, New Hampshire. The Arbor Room, the inn's premier accommodation, is located on the second floor overlooking the courtyard. It is beautifully decorated in blue and rose with a formal fireplace, two-person Jacuzzi, Victorian lace canopy and antique and replica mahogany furniture.

Guests are delighted, if not overwhelmed, by the delicious and plentiful gourmet breakfasts prepared and served in the dining room by a crackling fire or, in warmer months, on the porch over-looking the garden.

INNKEEPERS:	Joanne Nichols
ADDRESS:	400 Brackett Road
	Rye, New Hampshire 03870
TELEPHONE:	(603) 431-7010
E-MAIL:	arbor@gsinet.net
WEBSITE:	www.arborinn.com
ROOMS:	4 Rooms; 1 Suite; Private baths
CHILDREN:	Children welcome
ANIMALS:	Not allowed
HANDICAPPED:	Not handicapped accessible
DIETARY NEEDS:	Will accommodate guests' special dietary needs

Egg Blossoms

Makes 4 Servings

3	sheets phyllo dough, cut into 4 (4- to 5-inch) squares
4	tablespoons butter, melted
1	cup grated smoked Gouda cheese, divided
4	slices Canadian bacon or ham or 4 ounces smoked salmon, chopped and divided
3	cups chopped, stemmed fresh spinach, divided
4	eggs, divided

Salt and pepper, to taste
Paprika, for garnish
Fresh chive spears, for garnish

Preheat oven to 350°F. Spray large muffins cups with non-stick cooking spray. Press 1 square of phyllo into each cup; brush with melted butter. Sprinkle ¼ cup of cheese into each phyllo square. Top with 1 slice of Canadian bacon or 1 ounce of smoked salmon and of ¾ cup of spinach. Make a well in spinach and carefully crack 1 egg into well in each cup. Season with salt and pepper. Bake for 18 minutes. Remove from oven and let stand for 5 minutes. Carefully remove to plates. Top with Hollandaise sauce, sprinkle with a little paprika and top with a criss-cross of chives.

Hollandaise sauce:

4	egg yolks
1	tablespoon fresh lemon juice
1	stick butter, cut into pieces

In a small saucepan over low heat, whisk together egg yolks and lemon juice until combined. Add butter and cook, whisking constantly, until mixture thickens. If sauce is too thick, whisk in a little bit of water. Remove from heat and use immediately.

Galen C. Moses House

There are surprises throughout the Galen C. Moses House, from the elegant gardens and rooms filled with tasteful antiques to the full theatre located on the third floor (once used to entertain officers from the nearby Naval Air Station during World War II).

"This was our first b&b experience and I'm certain there will never be one as memorable and lovely. So many of your beautiful touches reminded me of my mother's things. The breakfasts were divine. I felt so spoiled by your service to us and by your talent in the kitchen." ~ Guests, North Carolina

INNKEEPERS:	Jim Haught & Larry Kieft
ADDRESS:	1009 Washington Street
	Bath, Maine 04530
TELEPHONE:	(207) 442-8771; (888) 442-8771
E-MAIL:	stay@galenmoses.com
WEBSITE:	www.galenmoses.com
ROOMS:	4 Rooms; 1 Suite; Private baths
CHILDREN:	Children age 13 and older welcome
ANIMALS:	Not allowed; Resident dog
HANDICAPPED:	Not handicapped accessible
DIETARY NEEDS:	Will accommodate guests' special dietary needs

Baked Eggs in Maple Toast Cups

Makes 4 Servings

- 2 tablespoons maple syrup
- 2 tablespoons butter
- 8 slices white bread, crusts removed
- 8 large eggs

Salt and pepper, to taste

Preheat oven to 400°F. Combine maple syrup and butter in a small saucepan over medium-low heat. Heat until butter is melted, then stir to combine. Roll out bread slices with a rolling pin until thin enough to press into a muffin cup. Brush each slice of bread with maple syrup mixture and press into greased muffin cups, maple syrup-side-up. Break 1 egg into each muffin cup. Sprinkle with salt and pepper. Bake for 15 minutes.

Inn Britannia

Nestled on five acres of gorgeous English gardens and dense woods, Inn Britannia offers the most bountiful gourmet breakfasts, the most elegant accommodations and the friendliest hosts on Mid-Coast Maine. Built in 1830, Inn Britannia is a historic, sea captain's home – lovingly restored, beautifully decorated and comfortably furnished with exquisite antiques.

The inn is central to all Maine coast activities and destinations. From Bar Harbor and Acadia to Camden and Boothbay Harbor, the inn is within an hour of whale watching, sailing, antiquing, shopping, hiking and skiing.

INNKEEPERS:	Caren Lorelle
ADDRESS:	132 West Main Street
	Searsport, Maine 04974
TELEPHONE:	(207) 548-2007; (866) 466-8142
E-MAIL:	info@innbritannia.com
WEBSITE:	www.innbritannia.com
ROOMS:	7 Rooms; 1 Suite; Private baths
CHILDREN:	Children age 12 and older welcome
ANIMALS:	Small pets welcome; Call ahead
HANDICAPPED:	Handicapped accessible; 1 Room
DIETARY NEEDS:	Will accommodate guests' special dietary needs

Cornish Baked Eggs

Makes 1 Serving

"This is our house specialty. It is a savory meringue that makes a very impressive presentation. Simply multiply the recipe for the given number of guests." - Innkeeper, Inn Britannia

Butter
½   English muffin, 1 slice bread or ½ biscuit
Grated Parmesan cheese
1   egg, separated
1   teaspoon chopped parsley
1   teaspoon chopped chives
1   teaspoon chopped fennel
Salt and pepper, to taste

Preheat oven to 350°F. Butter English muffin and sprinkle with Parmesan cheese. Put English muffin on a baking sheet (if making more than 1 serving, leave several inches between each English muffin).

Beat egg white until very stiff. Fold in chopped parsley, chives and fennel. Mound egg whites on English muffin (do not smooth edges). Gently place egg yolk in middle of egg whites and push yolk into whites to hold it in place. Sprinkle liberally with Parmesan cheese. Sprinkle lightly with salt and pepper. Bake for 10-14 minutes. Serve immediately.

The Parsonage Inn

Experience the essence of Cape Cod at the Parsonage Inn, a romantic inn nestled in the quiet village of East Orleans, just one and a half miles from Nauset Beach – the best beach on the Cape. Built around 1770, the inn is an authentic full-Cape house. In the 1800s, the building served as a vicarage; today it is a cozy, comfortable and romantic inn.

Guest rooms are Colonial in feel and are uniquely decorated with country antiques, quilts, stenciling and fresh flowers. Breakfasts change daily but never fail to delight and intrigue guests' palates.

INNKEEPERS:	Ian & Elizabeth Browne
ADDRESS:	202 Main Street
	East Orleans, Massachusetts 02643
TELEPHONE:	(508) 255-8217; (888) 422-8217
E-MAIL:	innkeeper@parsonageinn.com
WEBSITE:	www.parsonageinn.com
ROOMS:	8 Rooms; Private baths
CHILDREN:	Children age 6 and older welcome
ANIMALS:	Not allowed; Resident cat
HANDICAPPED:	Not handicapped accessible
DIETARY NEEDS:	Will accommodate guests' special dietary needs

Herb-Baked Eggs

Makes 4 Servings

"This recipe can be easily doubled or tripled. You can also make it the day before. Just cool, cover with foil and refrigerate, then reheat the eggs the next day in a preheated 300°F oven." ~ Innkeeper, Parsonage Inn

4	thin slices ham (optional)
3	large eggs
1	teaspoon Dijon mustard
¼	cup plain yogurt
¾	cup grated cheddar cheese, divided
2	teaspoons chopped chives, divided
2	teaspoons chopped fresh parsley, divided
1	green onion, sliced and divided

Toast, for serving
Fresh herb sprigs, for garnish

Preheat oven to 375°F. Line each of 4 greased muffin cups with 1 slice of ham. Beat together eggs, mustard and yogurt. Stir in ½ of cheese, 1 teaspoon of chopped chives, 1 teaspoon of chopped parsley and ½ of green onion. Divide egg mixture among muffin cups. Sprinkle with remaining cheese, chives, parsley and green onion. Bake for 25-30 minutes. Turn out onto serving plates. Serve with toast and fresh herb sprigs.

1794 Watchtide by the Sea

Located just a stone's throw from Searsport and a short drive to Acadia National Park, 1794 Watchtide by the Sea offers guests Mid-Coast Maine's finest accommodations. Overlooking beautiful, sparkling Penobscot Bay, this country inn is ideal for those seeking romance on the rock-bound coast, visiting the many fine galleries, museums and antique shops in Searsport or enjoying a whale-watching or sailing experience.

Awaken to an exquisitely prepared breakfast, served on the beautiful sun porch overlooking the bird sanctuary and Penobscot Bay.

INNKEEPERS:	Nancy-Linn Nellis
ADDRESS:	190 West Main Street
	Searsport, Maine, 04974
TELEPHONE:	(207) 548-6575; (800) 698-6575
E-MAIL:	stay@watchtide.com
WEBSITE:	www.watchtide.com
ROOMS:	3 Rooms; 2 Suites; Private baths
CHILDREN:	Children age 10 and older welcome
ANIMALS:	Not allowed
HANDICAPPED:	Not handicapped accessible
DIETARY NEEDS:	Will accommodate guests' special dietary needs

Savory Smoked Atlantic Salmon Clafoutti

Makes 6 Servings

"This recipe won the Blue Ribbon Award from Yankee Magazine." ~ Innkeeper, 1794 Watchtide by the Sea

½	stick unsalted butter
½-¾	cup chopped smoked salmon
3	plum tomatoes, juiced, seeded and chopped, plus sliced tomatoes, for serving
1½	cups grated Jarlsberg cheese
3	eggs, beaten
1	cup milk
¾	cup all-purpose flour

Dash of Tabasco sauce
1 teaspoon dill weed
1 teaspoon salt
½ teaspoon white pepper
Salad greens, for serving

Preheat oven to 375°F. Melt butter in a large, heavy cast-iron or oven-proof skillet, then remove from heat. Brush sides of skillet with butter. Scatter smoked salmon over bottom of skillet. Top with chopped tomatoes. Sprinkle cheese over tomatoes.

Whisk together eggs and milk. Stir in flour, Tabasco, dill, salt and pepper; slowly pour over ingredients in skillet. Put skillet in oven and bake for about 20 minutes, or until a toothpick inserted in center comes out clean. Let stand for about 5 minutes. Run a knife around edge of skillet to loosen clafoutti. Slice and serve with salad greens and sliced tomatoes.

The Winslow House

Elegant, wide board, pine floors, simple antique decor and a relaxed feel make The Winslow House a comfortable and charming destination. Rooms feature queen-size beds with country quilts or Italian bedding (and a down comforter when it gets chilly), specialty toiletries and Vermont maple candies.

The Winslow House is located in Woodstock, perennially voted one of the ten most picturesque towns in America. Quaint and elegant surroundings are reminiscent of an era when tradition, romance and simplicity prevailed.

INNKEEPERS:	Tod & Jen Minotti
ADDRESS:	492 Woodstock Road
	Woodstock, Vermont 05091
TELEPHONE:	(802) 457-1820 ; (866) 457-1820
E-MAIL:	info@thewinslowhousevt.com
WEBSITE:	www.thewinslowhousevt.com
ROOMS:	1 Rooms; 3 Suites; Private baths
CHILDREN:	Children age 8 and older welcome
ANIMALS:	Welcome; On-site boarding
HANDICAPPED:	Not handicapped accessible
DIETARY NEEDS:	Will accommodate guests' special dietary needs

Smoked Salmon & Artichoke Frittata

Makes 4 Servings

2	tablespoons olive oil
¼	cup chopped Vidalia onion (or other sweet onion)
½	cup chopped water-packed artichoke hearts
8	eggs
½	cup half & half
½	cup chopped smoked salmon
1	tablespoon chopped fresh dill

Salt and pepper, to taste

Preheat broiler. Heat oil in a 10-inch skillet over medium heat. Add onions and cook until mostly translucent. Stir in artichokes. Beat together eggs and half & half; pour evenly over onion mixture. Lower heat to low. Sprinkle with smoked salmon and dill. Season with salt and pepper.

Let frittata cook slowly from the bottom up. As edges become firm, gently lift edges with a spatula and allow uncooked egg to flow underneath into contact with skillet (this will help mixture cook evenly).

When frittata is about ¾-cooked (bottom is firm and top is still loose), put skillet in oven and bake frittata bake from the top down, checking often. When top is firm, and perhaps a little browned, remove from oven. Cool for about 1 minute, then slice and serve.

Addison Choate Inn

The Addison Choate Inn is an elegant, late Greek Revival home that has served as a bed & breakfast for almost 40 years. If you appreciate traditional decor and modern comforts, you will feel totally at home in the Addison Choate. Guests may relax with a book in the library or sip a cup of herbal tea in front of a roaring fire in the living room.

Breakfast is served in the fireplaced dining room during cool seasons and on the awning-shaded veranda in warm weather. Afternoon refreshments include home-baked cookies and a choice of seasonal beverages.

INNKEEPERS:	Cynthia Francis & Ed Cambron
ADDRESS:	49 Broadway
	Rockport, Massachusetts 01966
TELEPHONE:	(978) 546-7543; (800) 245-7543
E-MAIL:	info@addisonchoateinn.com
WEBSITE:	www.addisonchoateinn.com
ROOMS:	5 Rooms; 1 Suite; 2 Cottages; Private baths
CHILDREN:	Children age 12 and older welcome
ANIMALS:	Not allowed; Resident cat
HANDICAPPED:	Not handicapped accessible
DIETARY NEEDS:	Will accommodate guests' special dietary needs

Goat Cheese, Asparagus & Spring Onion Frittata

Makes 6 to 8 Servings

"This recipe can be adapted to use whatever vegetables you have on hand." - Innkeeper, Addison Choate Inn

1	tablespoon olive oil
1	cup diced asparagus, zucchini or summer squash
1	medium shallot, diced
8	large eggs, beaten
½	teaspoon sea salt
½	teaspoon freshly ground pepper
½	cup crumbled goat cheese
2	tablespoons thinly sliced spring onion (green onion)

Preheat oven to 400°F. Heat oil in an oven-proof, 10- to 12-inch skillet over medium-high heat. Add asparagus and shallots; cook until asparagus is crisp-tender and shallots are soft.

Combine eggs, salt and pepper; add to asparagus mixture and cook for about 2 minutes. Sprinkle goat cheese and spring onions over ingredients in skillet. Place skillet in oven and bake for 25 minutes. Cool slightly, then invert onto a serving platter. Slice and serve.

1831 Zachariah Eddy House

This award-winning bed & breakfast, listed in the National Register of Historic Places, offers comfortable elegance, tranquility, sumptuous breakfasts and lobster in season. Located within 35 miles of Boston, Cape Cod, Providence, Plymouth, Newport and the Martha's Vineyard ferry, the Eddy House is the perfect location for touring southern New England.

Lighthouse and sunset cruises, the Brimfield Outdoor Antique Show, whale watching, Plimoth Plantation, Newport mansions and Boston are just a few of the "101 things to do near the inn."

INNKEEPERS:	Bradford & Cheryl Leonard
ADDRESS:	51 South Main Street
	Middleboro, Massachusetts 02346
TELEPHONE:	(508) 946-0016
E-MAIL:	info@1831eddyhousebb.com
WEBSITE:	www.1831eddyhousebb.com
ROOMS:	3 Rooms; Private & shared baths
CHILDREN:	Children welcome; call ahead
ANIMALS:	Not allowed
HANDICAPPED:	Not handicapped accessible
DIETARY NEEDS:	Will accommodate guests' special dietary needs

Lobster Quiche

Makes 6 Servings

"Lobster is frequently served at breakfast and lobster quiche is always a favorite at the Eddy House." ~ Innkeeper, 1831 Zachariah Eddy House Bed & Breakfast

1	cup grated Monterey Jack cheese
1	(9-inch) deep-dish frozen pie crust
¾	stick butter
2	teaspoons minced garlic
2	cups cooked lobster meat, cut into 1-inch pieces (other seafood such as cooked shrimp, scallops or crab may be added and/or substituted in any combination)
2	teaspoons chopped fresh parsley
1	teaspoon dried tarragon

Salt and pepper, to taste

1	cup soft breadcrumbs
3	large eggs
1½	cups light cream or half & half
1	tablespoon grated Parmesan cheese

Paprika

Preheat oven to 375°F. Sprinkle Monterey Jack cheese over pie crust. Melt butter in a medium skillet over medium heat. Add garlic and cook for 1 minute. Add lobster, parsley, tarragon, salt and pepper. Lower heat to low and cook for 3-5 minutes, just long enough to blend ingredients. Remove from heat. Transfer lobster mixture to a large bowl and gently fold in breadcrumbs. Put lobster mixture in pie crust.

Whisk together eggs and cream; pour over lobster mixture. Place quiche in oven with a baking sheet underneath to catch any overflow. Bake for 30 minutes. Sprinkle with Parmesan cheese and a little paprika and bake for 15 minutes longer, or until a toothpick inserted in center comes out clean.

The Chadwick

The term "simple elegance" perfectly describes this Queen Anne-style bed & breakfast nestled in Portland's historic West End. Built in 1891, the Chadwick features a three-story turret and its original fireplaces. From the inn, it's a short walk to the Arts District, home to numerous galleries, theaters and the Portland Museum of Art. Also nearby is the city's lively old port, overflowing with fine shops and excellent restaurants.

Breakfast is served fireside in the formal dining room or, for the less formal, in the living room turret, the garden or delivered to your door.

INNKEEPERS:	Sarah deDoes
ADDRESS:	140 Chadwick Street
	Portland, Maine 04102
TELEPHONE:	(207) 774-5141; (800) 774-2137
E-MAIL:	chadwick@maine.rr.com
WEBSITE:	www.thechadwick.com
ROOMS:	4 Rooms; Private baths
CHILDREN:	Not allowed
ANIMALS:	Not allowed
HANDICAPPED:	Not handicapped accessible
DIETARY NEEDS:	Will accommodate guests' special dietary needs

Crab Quiche

Makes 6 Servings

8	ounces crabmeat
1	cup grated Swiss cheese
2	green onions, finely chopped
¼	cup sliced almonds
½	teaspoon grated lemon zest
1	(9-inch) pre-baked pie crust
4	large eggs
2	cups half & half
½	teaspoon salt
¼	teaspoon dry mustard

Dash of mace

Preheat oven to 425°F. Sprinkle crabmeat, cheese, green onions, almonds and lemon zest into crust. Combine eggs, half & half, salt, dry mustard and mace; pour over ingredients in crust. Bake for 15 minutes. Lower oven temperature to 300°F and bake for 30 minutes longer. Let stand for 10 minutes before slicing and serving.

Pryor House

Overlooking the Kennebec River in historic Bath, "the City of Ships," and just a few blocks from the heart of town, the Pryor House is nestled on a historic, tree-lined street that exudes historic elegance and charm. A full breakfast is served in the dining room and includes an array of fresh ingredients and house specialties.

After a day of hiking, shopping or visiting one of the many nearby colleges, relax in the Jacuzzi with a bottle of sparkling cider or Champagne.

INNKEEPERS:	Don & Gwenda Pryor
ADDRESS:	360 Front Street
	Bath, Maine 04530
TELEPHONE:	(207) 443-1146
E-MAIL:	pryorhse@suscommaine.com
WEBSITE:	home.gwi.net/~pryorhse (no 'www')
ROOMS:	3 Rooms; Private baths
CHILDREN:	Children age 12 and older welcome
ANIMALS:	Not allowed
HANDICAPPED:	Not handicapped accessible
DIETARY NEEDS:	Will accommodate guests' special dietary needs

Pryor House Sausage Quiche

Makes 6 to 8 Servings

Crust:
- 3 cups all-purpose flour
- 1 cup plus 1½ tablespoons shortening
- 1½ teaspoons salt
- 1 egg
- ⅓ cup ice water
- 1 teaspoon cider vinegar

Filling:
- 1½ teaspoons butter
- ¼ cup chopped onion
- 8 ounces bulk pork sausage, cooked (or chopped tomato and oregano, or whatever you want to add)
- 1 cup grated Swiss cheese
- 1 cup grated cheddar cheese
- 3 eggs, beaten
- 1¼ cups light cream or milk
- ¾ teaspoon salt
- ⅛ teaspoon pepper

For the crust: Preheat oven to 350°F. In a large bowl, cut together flour, shortening and salt. In a small bowl, beat together egg, water and vinegar; add to flour mixture and stir until a ball forms. Roll out dough and fit in a 9-inch pie pan; flute edges (do not prick crust). Bake for 7 minutes.

For the filling: Melt butter in a small skillet over medium heat. Add onions and cook until soft; cool slightly. Layer sausage, onion and cheddar and Swiss cheese in crust. Combine eggs, cream, salt and pepper; pour over ingredients in crust. Bake for 30-35 minutes, or until set. Let stand for 10 minutes, then slice and serve.

Colby Hill Inn

The Colby Hill Inn is located right in the middle of southern New Hampshire. Henniker is just 90 minutes north of Boston and 20 minutes west of Concord, the state capital. The inn is just an hour from the seashore and minutes from New Hampshire's mountains and lakes. Guest rooms are individually decorated and have luxury bedding. Some rooms feature fireplaces, two-person whirlpool tubs and canopy beds.

The Colby Hill Inn was awarded The Wine Spectator Award of Excellence and 2003 *Yankee Magazine* Editors' Pick.

INNKEEPERS:	Cyndi & Mason Cobb
ADDRESS:	3 The Oaks
	Henniker, New Hampshire 03242
TELEPHONE:	(603) 428-3281; (800) 531-0330
E-MAIL:	innkeeper@colbyhillinn.com
WEBSITE:	www.colbyhillinn.com
ROOMS:	13 Rooms; 2 Suites; Private baths
CHILDREN:	Children age 7 and older welcome
ANIMALS:	Not allowed
HANDICAPPED:	Limited; Call ahead
DIETARY NEEDS:	Will accommodate guests' special dietary needs

Potato Pancakes with Poached Eggs & Cheddar

Makes 8 Servings

"For variety, try topping the potato pancakes with chopped tomato, roasted red bell pepper, spinach or broccoli before adding the poached eggs and cheese." ~ Innkeeper, Colby Hill Inn

6	large potatoes, peeled and grated
1	large onion, grated
¾	cup all-purpose flour
2-3	large eggs, beaten, plus 8 eggs, poached

Salt and pepper, to taste

¾   cup grated cheddar cheese (or Swiss, crumbled feta, etc.)

Combine potatoes, onion, flour and beaten eggs (start with 2 eggs and add a third, if needed to achieve desired consistency). Form potato mixture into cakes and cook on an oiled or buttered griddle or skillet over medium-high heat until golden brown on both sides. Top pancakes with a poached egg and a little cheese. If desired, serve on oven-proof plates and place plates in a 350°F oven until cheese is melted.

Captain Briggs House

A beautifully restored 1853 shipbuilder's home, the Captain Briggs House Bed & Breakfast is located on a quiet side street, just three blocks from L.L. Bean and within easy walking distance of Freeport's many fine shops and restaurants. Spend a day visiting lighthouses and museums or hiking trails in coastal parks. Scenic cruises offer fine opportunities to see Maine's coastline and wildlife.

"Thank you for your warm hospitality, comfortable room and the best breakfast we had on our entire trip!" ~ Guests, Tennessee

INNKEEPERS:	Celia & Rob Elberfeld
ADDRESS:	8 Maple Avenue
	Freeport, Maine 04032
TELEPHONE:	(207) 865-1868; (888) 217-2477
E-MAIL:	info@captainbriggs.com
WEBSITE:	www.captainbriggs.com
ROOMS:	6 Rooms; 1 Suite; Private baths
CHILDREN:	Call ahead
ANIMALS:	Not allowed
HANDICAPPED:	Not handicapped accessible
DIETARY NEEDS:	Will accommodate guests' special dietary needs

Lobster Breakfast Treat

Makes 6 Servings

"A flavorful and unique way to serve lobster for breakfast – our guests love it."
~ Innkeeper, Captain Briggs House Bed & Breakfast

2	tablespoons butter
2	tablespoons all-purpose flour
2½	cups whole milk
18	ounces fresh spinach, washed and chopped
¼	teaspoon ground coriander
1	cup lobster bisque
1	cup grated mild cheddar cheese
18	frozen lobster ravioli
6	extra-large or jumbo eggs
6	slices bread, toasted

Paprika, for garnish
6   edible flowers, for garnish

Melt butter in a saucepan over low heat. Stir in flour and cook, stirring, for 5 minutes, until mixture begins to bubble. Slowly whisk in milk, a little at a time. Cook for 15 minutes, until thickened.

In a saucepan, combine ½ of milk mixture and spinach; set aside. In a separate saucepan over low heat, combine remaining milk mixture with coriander, lobster bisque and cheddar cheese; heat slowly until cheese is melted and combined. Set aside and keep warm.

Cook lobster ravioli according to package directions. Heat spinach mixture. Poach eggs in boiling water with 1 tablespoon of white vinegar (helps keep eggs together).

Divide spinach mixture among serving plates. Top with 3 lobster ravioli and some of the lobster bisque mixture. Sprinkle with a little paprika. Put toast next to spinach and top with 1 poached egg. Garnish with a flower.

1 Murray House

One Murray House offers lovely guest rooms with full or half canopy beds, private baths and private outside entrances. A gourmet breakfast is served either in your room or on your private patio. The second level guest room has a panoramic view of Almy Pond and a distant ocean view.

For recreation, stroll Newport's famous waterfront and watch million-dollar yachts bob alongside ancient lobster boats. Enjoy world-class restaurants and walk the "Cliff Walk," a trail with unparalleled ocean views.

INNKEEPERS:	Noreen O'Neil
ADDRESS:	1 Murray Place
	Newport, Rhode Island 02840
TELEPHONE:	(401) 846-3337; (800) 773 5797
E-MAIL:	murrayhousebnb@aol.com
WEBSITE:	www.murrayhouse.com
ROOMS:	2 Rooms; 1 Suite; Private baths
CHILDREN:	Infants or children age 10 and older welcome
ANIMALS:	Welcome; Call ahead; Resident cats & dog
HANDICAPPED:	Not handicapped accessible
DIETARY NEEDS:	Will accommodate guests' special dietary needs

Ham & Potato Pie

Makes 6 to 8 Servings

"This dish can be prepared ahead and frozen." ~ Innkeeper, 1 Murray House Bed & Breakfast

1	cup diced cooked ham
3	hash brown patties, crumbled
1	cup chopped red, green and/or yellow bell peppers
½	cup chopped onion
2	cups grated cheddar cheese, divided
3	cups milk
1	cup Bisquick
4	eggs
1	teaspoon salt

Dash of pepper
1   heaping tablespoon chopped fresh parsley

Preheat oven to 375°F. Spray a 9x13-inch baking pan with non-stick cooking spray. Combine ham, hash browns, bell peppers, onion and 1 cup of cheese; spread over bottom of pan.

Combine milk, Bisquick, eggs, salt and pepper until well blended; pour over ham mixture in baking dish. Sprinkle with remaining 1 cup of cheese and parsley. Cover and refrigerate for 1 hour. Bake for 40-45 minutes, or until light golden brown around edges.

Grunberg Haus

Warmly welcoming guests since 1972, the Grunberg Haus is a beautiful Austrian chalet, hand-built like a country inn hidden in the Alps and set among towering pines and sugar maple trees. Escape into the countryside and enjoy quiet relaxation in a mountainside setting midway between the resorts of Stowe and Sugarbush.

Breakfast features homemade breads and hearty entrées. Gaze out a 20-foot glass wall and watch wildlife while you savor pumpkin apple streusel muffins, maple-poached pears and ricotta-stuffed French toast.

INNKEEPERS:	Linda & Jeff Connor
ADDRESS:	94 Pine Street, Route 100 South
	Waterbury, Vermont 05676
TELEPHONE:	(802) 244-7726; (800) 800-7760
E-MAIL:	info@grunberghaus.com
WEBSITE:	www.grunberghaus.com
ROOMS:	9 Rooms; 2 Suites; 3 Cottages; Private & shared baths
CHILDREN:	Children age 5 and older welcome
ANIMALS:	Dogs & cats welcome in cabins
HANDICAPPED:	Not handicapped accessible
DIETARY NEEDS:	Will accommodate guests' special dietary needs

Vermont Cheddar Pie

Makes 6 Servings

"Our specialty is Vermont cheddar pie, made of freshly gathered eggs and stuffed with genuine Vermont Cabot cheddar cheese. We serve the pie with lemon bread baked from an heirloom recipe and a fresh fruit sundae. ~ Innkeeper, Grunberg Haus Vermont Bed & Breakfast and Cabins

2	cups frozen hash browns, thawed
1	medium onion, finely chopped
1	teaspoon seasoned pepper
1	teaspoon garlic powder
1/3	cup grated Romano cheese
1/3	cup chopped spinach
1/4	cup crumbled feta cheese
1/3	cup grated Vermont sharp cheddar cheese (preferable Cabot)
2	large eggs
1/2	cup milk
2	tablespoons dried parsley flakes
2	teaspoons paprika

Red salsa, for serving

Preheat oven to 325°F. Spray a 9-inch glass pie pan with non-stick cooking spray. Combine hash browns and onions (reserve 2 tablespoons of onion for topping pie); press into pie pan to form a crust. Sprinkle with pepper, garlic powder and Romano cheese. Dot with spinach, then with feta cheese. Sprinkle with cheddar cheese.

Beat together eggs and milk; pour over pie, working from edges to middle. Place reserved 2 tablespoons of chopped onion in center of pie. Sprinkle parsley in a ring around onion, then sprinkle paprika around parsley to make an outer ring. Bake for about 1 hour, until lightly browned. Cut pie into 6 slices and serve with salsa.

Moses Nickerson House Inn

Whaling Captain Moses Nickerson built the Moses Nickerson House for his bride in 1839. They raised eight children in the rambling white house near Chatham Harbor. Innkeepers Linda and George Watts restored the house, creating an abode of simple elegance and romance. Wide pine floors and original glass windows – held open by notched sticks – echo a bygone era.

Breakfast is served in the glass-enclosed dining area which opens onto gracefully landscaped gardens with a water fountain and pond.

INNKEEPERS:	Linda & George Watts
ADDRESS:	364 Old Harbor Road
	Chatham, Massachusetts 02633
TELEPHONE:	(508) 945-5859; (800) 628-6972
E-MAIL:	tmnhi@comcast.net
WEBSITE:	www.mosesnickersonhouse.com
ROOMS:	7 Rooms; Private baths
CHILDREN:	Children age 10 and older welcome
ANIMALS:	Not allowed
HANDICAPPED:	Not handicapped accessible
DIETARY NEEDS:	Will accommodate guests' special dietary needs

Nantucket Pie

Makes 14 Servings

2	tablespoons vegetable oil
¾	cup chopped onion
10	cups shredded hash browns, thawed
20	large eggs
¾	cup milk
2⅓	cups grated cheddar cheese
1¾	cups grated mozzarella cheese
2	tablespoons dried parsley flakes
1	teaspoon pepper
2	teaspoons salt
12	slices bacon, cooked and chopped

Preheat oven to 350°F. Heat oil in a large skillet over medium heat. Add onions and hash browns; cook until onions are soft. Spread hash brown mixture in bottom of a greased 9x13-inch baking pan. Combine eggs, milk, cheeses, parsley flakes, pepper and salt; pour over hash browns. Sprinkle with bacon. Bake for 40 minutes.

Side Dishes, Soups & Salads

Indian Summer Corn Cakes 163

Indian Pudding 165

Pumpkin Yogurt 167

Potluck Potatoes 169

Garlic Chive Potato Pancakes 171

Flying Cloud Breakfast Sausage Patties 173

Cranberry & Pecan-Filled Squash 175

New England Lobster Bisque 177

Lobster Gazpacho 179

Maple Pumpkin Bisque 181

Curried Vermont Apple Soup 183

Roasted Red Pepper Soup..185

Easy Potato Leek Soup 187

Wauwinet Lobster "Cobb" Salad 189

Turkey, Apple & Pecan Salad 191

Side Dishes, Salads & Soups

Birchwood Inn

Kennedy Park, adjacent to the Birchwood Inn, boasts hundreds of acres of wooded trails for hiking, biking, cross-country skiing or snow shoeing. Golf, tennis, downhill skiing and water sports are also close at hand. Lenox, in the heart of the Berkshires, is the locale of Tanglewood, the summer home of the Boston Symphony Orchestra, as well as Shakespeare & Co. and the Norman Rockwell Museum.

Inn rooms are named after previous residents of the mansion, dating back to 1767. Deluxe rooms feature fireplaces, featherbeds and four poster beds.

INNKEEPERS:	Ellen Gutman Chenaux
ADDRESS:	7 Hubbard Street
	Lenox, Massachusetts 01240
TELEPHONE:	(413) 637-2600; (800) 524-1646
E-MAIL:	innkeeper@birchwood-inn.com
WEBSITE:	www.birchwood-inn.com
ROOMS:	10 Rooms; 1 Suite; Private baths
CHILDREN:	Children age 12 and older welcome
ANIMALS:	Not allowed; Resident dog
HANDICAPPED:	Not handicapped accessible
DIETARY NEEDS:	Will accommodate guests' special dietary needs

Indian Summer Corn Cakes

Makes 6 to 8 Servings

2	cups fresh or frozen (thawed) corn
1	(4-ounce) can chopped mild green chiles
1	tablespoon finely chopped cilantro
2	cloves garlic, minced
1	red bell pepper, diced
6	green onions, thinly sliced
2	large eggs
1¼	cups all-purpose flour
½	cup cornmeal
1	teaspoon baking powder
1	teaspoon kosher salt
2	tablespoons lime juice
1½	cups milk

Salt and freshly ground pepper, to taste

½ cup sour cream

Milk

¼ cup vegetable oil

Salsa, for serving

If using fresh corn, fill a saucepan ¾-full with water and bring to a boil. Add corn and cook for 1 minute; drain. If using thawed frozen corn, fill a saucepan ¼-full with water and bring to a boil. Add frozen corn and cook for 30 seconds; drain. Put corn in a large bowl; cool. Stir in cilantro, chiles, garlic, bell pepper and green onions. In a medium bowl, mix eggs, flour, cornmeal, baking powder, salt and lime juice just until combined. Add egg mixture to corn mixture; stir just until combined. Season with salt and pepper. Let batter stand at room temperature for 45-60 minutes.

Spoon sour cream into a squirt bottle (or in a dish). Thin it with a little milk. Heat oil in a large skillet or griddle over medium heat. Spoon batter onto griddle to form 4-inch cakes. Cook corn cakes for about 5 minutes, turning once, until golden brown on each side. Drain on paper towels. Drizzle thinned sour cream over cakes and serve with salsa on the side.

Shelter Harbor Inn

Built in the early 1800s, the Shelter Harbor Inn has been transformed into a comfortable, unpretentious country inn where the emphasis is on relaxation, good food and a warm, friendly atmosphere. The inn sits at the entrance to Shelter Harbor and is near one of the most beautiful sections of Rhode Island's shoreline. The inn's private beach stretches for two miles along the shores of Quonochontaug Pond and the ocean.

Each day, the inn's chef prepares creative American cuisine using only the freshest of ingredients and seafood from local waters.

INNKEEPERS:	Jim Dey
ADDRESS:	10 Wagner Road
	Westerly, Rhode Island 02891
TELEPHONE:	(401) 322-8883; (800) 468-8883
E-MAIL:	shelterharborinn@cox.net
WEBSITE:	www.shelterharborinn.com
ROOMS:	24 Rooms; Private baths
CHILDREN:	Welcome
ANIMALS:	Not allowed
HANDICAPPED:	Handicapped accessible
DIETARY NEEDS:	Will accommodate guests' special dietary needs

Indian Pudding

Makes 6 to 8 Servings

4	cups milk
2	cups heavy cream
1	cup molasses
¾	cup white cornmeal
½	cup packed brown sugar
1	tablespoon butter
1	tablespoon cinnamon
1	tablespoon ground ginger
1½	teaspoons salt

Ice cream, for serving

Preheat oven to 350°F. Bring milk, cream and molasses to a boil in a heavy saucepan over medium-high heat. Stir in cornmeal, brown sugar, butter, cinnamon, ginger and salt. Lower heat and simmer, stirring frequently, for 5 minutes. Pour pudding into a well-greased 9x13-inch baking dish. Put baking dish in a 12x18-inch baking pan. Add enough hot water to come halfway up sides of baking dish. Bake for 60 minutes, stirring with a whisk or a wooden spoon for 1 minute every 15 minutes, until firm to the touch. Remove from oven. Cool for 15-20 minutes. Serve warm with ice cream.

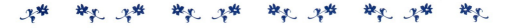

Lovejoy Farm

Located on a quiet country road and surrounded by acres of fields and woods, Lovejoy Farm in an elegant, 1790 Georgian Colonial complete with beamed ceilings for rustic charm. The decor and furnishings reflect the antiquity of a bygone era with Oriental rugs, original stenciled rooms and antique furniture. Built by one of the Loudon's founding fathers, the house has been painstakingly restored and renovated with an eye for detail.

Hearty country breakfasts feature homemade baked goods and pancakes and waffles served with the inn's own maple syrup.

INNKEEPERS:	Art Monty & Rena Simard
ADDRESS:	268 Lovejoy Road
	Loudon, New Hampshire 03307
TELEPHONE:	(603) 783-4007; (888) 783-4007
E-MAIL:	info@lovejoy-inn.com
WEBSITE:	www.lovejoy-inn.com
ROOMS:	8 Rooms; Private baths
CHILDREN:	Welcome
ANIMALS:	Dogs & cats welcome; Resident cat
HANDICAPPED:	Not handicapped accessible
DIETARY NEEDS:	Will accommodate guests' special dietary needs

Pumpkin Yogurt

Makes 12 Servings

"None of our guests had ever had this rich yogurt before staying with us. I serve it with sliced bananas and our maple syrup, which we make the old-fashioned way – wood cooked and heated." - Innkeeper, Lovejoy Farm Bed & Breakfast

¾	cup sugar
½	teaspoon salt
1	tablespoon plus ¾ teaspoon cinnamon
½	teaspoon ground ginger
½	teaspoon ground cloves
½	teaspoon allspice
2	large eggs
1	(16-ounce) can pumpkin pie filling
1	(14-ounce) can sweetened condensed milk
⅓	cup pure maple syrup
1	(32-ounce) container plain whole milk yogurt (Stony Field is good)

Sliced bananas, for serving
Yogurt cream or sweetened whipped cream, for serving*

Preheat oven to 350°F. In a small bowl, combine sugar, salt, cinnamon, ginger, cloves and allspice. In a 1½-quart casserole dish, beat eggs lightly. Stir in pumpkin and sugar mixture. Gradually beat in condensed milk.

Set casserole dish in a deep baking pan. Add enough hot water to come halfway up sides of casserole dish. Bake for 1 hour. Cool, then stir in maple syrup and yogurt. Cover and chill for at least 3 hours. Serve with sliced bananas and yogurt cream, if desired. This dish freezes very well.

*Note: Yogurt cream is made by combining 1 cup well-chilled heavy cream, 2½ tablespoons powdered sugar and ½ cup plain yogurt.

Honeysuckle Hill

At Honeysuckle Hill, breakfast is served in the sunny dining room. The menu changes daily and offers such gourmet treats as Dutch babies, the Captain's eggs or Grand Marnier French toast. Rooms are delightfully furnished with antiques, white wicker and featherbeds. Each room has a private bath with an oversized marble shower, fresh flowers, English toiletries and terry cloth robes.

"Your warmth and hospitality goes beyond words, not to mention the fabulous breakfasts and exceptional conversation." ~ Guests, Honeysuckle Hill

INNKEEPERS:	Bill & Mary Kilburn
ADDRESS:	591 Main Street, Route 6A
	West Barnstable, Massachusetts 02668
TELEPHONE:	(508) 362-8418
E-MAIL:	stay@honeysucklehill.com
WEBSITE:	www.honeysucklehill.com
ROOMS:	3 Rooms; 1 Suite; Private baths
CHILDREN:	Welcome
ANIMALS:	Not allowed
HANDICAPPED:	Not handicapped accessible
DIETARY NEEDS:	Will accommodate guests' special dietary needs

Potluck Potatoes

Makes 12 to 16 Servings

"This is a wonderful dish to take along when you are asked to bring something to the dinner party. It's easy to make and travels well. Expect to take home an empty dish!" ~ Innkeeper, Honeysuckle Hill Bed & Breakfast

2	(10¾-ounce) cans condensed cream of potato soup
1	cup sour cream
½	teaspoon garlic salt
1	(32-ounce) package frozen hash browns, thawed
2	cups grated cheddar cheese
½	cup grated Parmesan cheese

Preheat oven to 350°F. Combine soup, sour cream and garlic salt. Add hash browns and cheddar cheese; mix well. Pour into a greased 9x13-inch baking pan. Sprinkle with Parmesan cheese. Bake for 55-60 minutes, or until potatoes are tender and top is lightly browned.

Mt. Chocorua View House

Warm and cozy in winter and cool and breezy in summer, this "mountain casual" country inn invites guests to relax in front of the fire or meander through the surrounding woods to the scenic Chocorua River. Located minutes from the Barnstormers, the oldest summer theater in New Hampshire, the inn offers hiking, biking, skiing, swimming, antiquing and shopping.

Linger over breakfast in the dining room, on the deck or on one of the porches. Bag lunches are available for daily excursions or the trip home.

INNKEEPERS:	Frank & Barb Holmes
ADDRESS:	Route 16
	Chocorua, New Hampshire 03817
TELEPHONE:	(603) 323-8350; (888) 323-8350
E-MAIL:	info@mtchocorua.com
WEBSITE:	www.mtchocorua.com
ROOMS:	7 Rooms; 1 Suite; Private & shared baths
CHILDREN:	Children age 10 and older welcome
ANIMALS:	Not allowed
HANDICAPPED:	Not handicapped accessible
DIETARY NEEDS:	Will accommodate guests' special dietary needs

Garlic Chive Potato Pancakes

Makes 8 to 10 Servings

"When served with sour cream and homemade applesauce, this makes a great vegetarian entrée. It is perfect for those allergic to wheat. Plan ahead – this dish needs to be started the night before." ~ Innkeeper, Mt. Chocorua View House

3	pounds potatoes (Yukon Gold are especially good), peeled and quartered
½	(8-ounce) package regular or low-fat cream cheese, softened
1	tablespoon chopped fresh chives
1	clove garlic, minced

Salt and pepper, to taste
Milk or half & half

Cook potatoes in salted boiling water until tender; drain and mash. Add cream cheese, chives, garlic, salt and pepper; beat until smooth. Add enough milk or half & half to make a creamy consistency. Cover and refrigerate overnight.

The next day, form potatoes into patties, using ¼-⅓ cup of potatoes per patty. Cook patties on a preheated, greased or buttered griddle or a skillet until heated through and golden brown on both sides.

The Flying Cloud

Between 1838 and 1840, sea captain George Washington Tukey built a Greek Revival addition to an old 1790 Cape Cod house, making a home for his bride. The home is named for the elegant clipper ship the Flying Cloud. Launched in 1851, she set a speed record on her maiden voyage from the East Coast to the gold fields of the West Coast. Traveling around Cape Horn, she arrived in California in 89 days and 8 hours.

"Wonderful in every way! Such special personal touches. Thanks so much! We'll be back." ~ Guests, The Flying Cloud Bed & Breakfast

INNKEEPERS:	Dave & Karen Bragg
ADDRESS:	45 River Road
	Newcastle, Maine 04553
TELEPHONE:	(207) 563-2484
E-MAIL:	stay@theflyingcloud.com
WEBSITE:	www.theflyingcloud.com
ROOMS:	5 Rooms; 1 Suite; Private baths
CHILDREN:	Children age 10 and older welcome
ANIMALS:	Not allowed
HANDICAPPED:	Not handicapped accessible
DIETARY NEEDS:	Will accommodate guests' special dietary needs

Flying Cloud Breakfast Sausage Patties

Makes 26 Patties or 1 Loaf

"This is our most requested recipe. It can be made into individual patties and frozen. Just pull out the number you need for breakfast. It can also be made as a loaf for a crowd." ~ Innkeeper, The Flying Cloud Bed & Breakfast

1½	pounds bulk sausage (such as Jimmy Dean's reduced fat sausage)
1	cup grated apple
1	tablespoon chopped fresh sage
1	small onion, minced
2	tablespoons chopped fresh parsley
⅔	cup dry breadcrumbs
½	teaspoon chopped fresh rosemary
2	eggs, lightly beaten
½	teaspoon pepper
1	tablespoon Maine maple syrup
½	teaspoon kosher salt
⅛	teaspoon cayenne pepper, or to taste

Combine all ingredients in order given and mix well. (If freezing, drop mixture by generous tablespoonful onto a waxed paper-lined cookie sheet. Freeze completely, then seal in freezer bags and label with date.)

For patties: Shape sausage mixture into patties. Heat just enough olive oil to keep patties from sticking in a skillet over medium-high heat. Cook patties for 3 minutes per side. Add 2-3 tablespoons of water to skillet and cook until patties are cooked through, about 10-15 minutes, depending on thickness of patties. Serve 2 patties per person

For a loaf: Preheat oven to 350°F. Spray a 4x8-inch loaf pan with non-stick cooking spray. Put sausage mixture in pan. Bake for 1 hour, or until internal temperature is 165-170°F. Remove loaf from pan to a platter. Let stand for 5 minutes before slicing. Makes 10-12 slices.

The Blue Hill Inn

Visit Blue Hill, a quiet and scenic place on the coast where you can sail, cruise or kayak past the lighthouses of Penobscot Bay, shop for antiques or attend a chamber music concert. Then return to the Blue Hill Inn, a place of distinction where wine and hors d'oeuvres are served fireside and the priority is individualized guest attention.

Breakfast may include blueberry pancakes, Amaretto French toast, Belgian waffles with strawberries and Brie and roasted red pepper omelets. Locally raised ingredients, including Maine maple syrup, are featured.

INNKEEPERS:	Mary & Don Hartley
ADDRESS:	40 Union Street
	Blue Hill, Maine 04614
TELEPHONE:	(207) 374-2844; (800) 826-7415
E-MAIL:	mary@bluehillinn.com
WEBSITE:	www.bluehillinn.com
ROOMS:	10 Rooms; 2 Suites; Private baths
CHILDREN:	Welcome
ANIMALS:	Not allowed
HANDICAPPED:	Handicapped accessible
DIETARY NEEDS:	Will accommodate guests' special dietary needs

Cranberry & Pecan-Filled Squash

Makes 4 Servings

"Cranberries and pecans turn squash into a festive holiday dish." - Innkeeper, The Blue Hill Inn

2	tablespoons unsalted butter
¾	cup pecan halves or large pieces
2	medium delicata or sweet dumpling squash, washed, halved and cavities scraped clean
¼	teaspoon cinnamon
3	small bunches baby bok choy, sliced into ½-inch-thick slices
¾	cup dried cranberries

Preheat oven to 350°F. Melt butter in a small skillet over low heat. Add pecans and cook just until golden; set aside.

Sprinkle each squash half with cinnamon. Combine bok choy, cranberries and pecans; stuff in cavities of squash halves. Place squash, cut-side-up, in a baking dish (do not crowd). Pour ½-inch of water in baking dish and cover with foil. Bake for about 30 minutes, or until squash pierces easily with a fork. Serve hot.

Roger Sherman Inn

The circa 1740 Roger Sherman Inn is a restored Colonial landmark, located near the center of New Canaan and its fashionable shops and historic sites. The inn is named for Roger Sherman, a lawyer and delegate to the Continental Congress who was a signer of the Declaration of Independence and the United States Constitution.

The inn offers quiet surroundings, seasonal outdoor dining, a well-stocked wine cellar and award-winning, contemporary Continental cuisine. The menu features daily, seasonal offerings, fresh seafood and Swiss specialties.

INNKEEPERS:	Thomas Weilenmann
ADDRESS:	195 Oenoke Ridge
	New Canaan, Connecticut 06840
TELEPHONE:	(203) 966-4541
E-MAIL:	info@rogershermaninn.com
WEBSITE:	www.rogershermaninn.com
ROOMS:	16 Rooms; 1 Suite; Private baths
CHILDREN:	Children welcome
ANIMALS:	Not allowed
HANDICAPPED:	Call ahead
DIETARY NEEDS:	Call ahead

New England Lobster Bisque

Makes 4 Servings

4	(1½-pound) lobster culls
¼	cup soy oil (vegetable oil will work as well – do not use olive oil)
2	ounces carrots, peeled and diced into small cubes
2	ounces celery root, peeled and diced into small cubes
4	ounces shallots, diced into small cubes
2	ounces leeks, cleaned and diced into small cubes
2	ounces potatoes, peeled and diced into small cubes
¼	cup tomato purée
¼	cup cognac
1	cup white wine
6	cups clam juice
½	bunch tarragon
2	bay leaves
3	juniper berries
2	cups heavy cream

Salt, to taste

Separate lobster tails and claws from heads and thoroughly clean inner parts (keep all lobster parts). Heat oil in a soup pot over medium-high heat; add lobster parts and cook just until they begin to turn red. Add carrots, celery root and shallots; cook until tender. Add leeks and potatoes; cook for 5-10 minutes, or until golden brown. Add tomato purée, stirring constantly (do not let tomato purée turn brown – it will make the bisque bitter). Add cognac and white wine. Lower heat to low and simmer until most of alcohol is cooked off. Add clam juice and simmer for about 5 minutes. Add tarragon, bay leaves and juniper berries.

Remove all lobster shell parts from soup. Separate lobster meat from shell; set lobster meat aside and keep warm. Slowly simmer soup over medium heat for about 20 minutes. Add cream. Purée soup in blender. Strain through a fine sieve. Season with salt, if needed. Pour soup into bowls and top with lobster meat to serve.

*Note: Lobster culls are lobsters missing a claw, often sold at a lower price.

Rabbit Hill Inn

The AAA Four-Diamond, Mobil Four-Star Rabbit Hill Inn sits peacefully upon 15 acres of unspoiled countryside in the time-forgotten village of Lower Waterford in the Northeast Kingdom of Vermont. A glance south captures majestic views of the White Mountains. A stroll past the white steeple church takes you to the Connecticut River.

Dining at the Rabbit Hill Inn is unsurpassed. Enjoy glorious breakfasts by candlelight and celebrate your evenings with five courses of delectable, award-winning New American Cuisine – all included with your room!

INNKEEPERS:	Brian & Leslie Mulcahy
ADDRESS:	48 Lower Waterford Road
	Lower Waterford, Vermont 05848
TELEPHONE:	(802) 748-5168; (800) 762-8669
E-MAIL:	info@rabbithillinn.com
WEBSITE:	www.rabbithillinn.com
ROOMS:	11 Rooms; 8 Suites; Private baths
CHILDREN:	Children age 13 and older welcome
ANIMALS:	Not allowed
HANDICAPPED:	Handicapped accessible
DIETARY NEEDS:	Will accommodate guests' special dietary needs

Lobster Gazpacho

Makes 4 Servings

Serve this elegant gazpacho with Blue & Yellow Cornmeal Pound Cake (see recipe on page 21).

Gazpacho:

4	slices white bread, diced
2	teaspoons minced garlic
⅓	cup sherry vinegar
10	tomatoes, seeded and chopped
½	cup olive oil
3	cups tomato juice

Salt and pepper, to taste

2	cups diced cooked lobster meat
1	cup finely diced vegetables, such as yellow and red bell peppers, cucumbers, carrots, zucchini, etc.

Scallion cream topping:

1	cup sour cream
¾	teaspoon minced garlic
1½	teaspoons lemon juice
¼	cup minced green onion
½	teaspoon pepper
1	teaspoon salt

For the gazpacho: Soak bread in water to cover for 15 minutes. Strain bread and transfer to a blender along with garlic, vinegar, tomatoes and olive oil. Purée (strain, if desired). Stir in tomato juice, salt and pepper. Cover and chill thoroughly.

Divide lobster meat and diced vegetables among bowls. Ladle 1 cup of gazpacho into each bowl. Top with scallion cream to serve.

For the scallion cream: Mix all topping ingredients.

Arlington's West Mountain Inn

Nestled on a mountainside, the century-old West Mountain Inn invites guests to discover its many treasures. Distinctively decorated guest rooms and comfortable common areas, along with 150 woodland acres with wildflowers, a bird sanctuary and llamas, provide space to relax and rejuvenate the body and spirit.

Miles of wilderness skiing or hiking trails and the Battenkill River provide seasonal outdoor activities. A hearty breakfast, complete with apple pie, and a fine country dinner in front of an open hearth, complement your stay.

INNKEEPERS:	The Carlson Family
ADDRESS:	144 River Road
	Arlington, Vermont 05250
TELEPHONE:	(802) 375-6516
E-MAIL:	info@westmountaininn.com
WEBSITE:	www.westmountaininn.com
ROOMS:	15 Rooms; 7 Suites; Private baths
CHILDREN:	Children welcome
ANIMALS:	Not allowed; Resident dog
HANDICAPPED:	Handicapped accessible
DIETARY NEEDS:	Will accommodate guests' special dietary needs

Maple Pumpkin Bisque

Makes 4 to 6 Servings

"Since we live in Vermont, maple syrup is often our sweetener of choice. In this soup, the pumpkin and maple flavors blend very well. The creamy orange color and the cinnamon and nutmeg really say fall." – Innkeeper, Arlington's West Mountain Inn

2	tablespoons vegetable oil
½	large red onion, chopped
1-2	cloves garlic, minced
½	medium pie pumpkin, peeled and diced
¾	cup Marsala wine
4	cups vegetable stock or broth
4	cups chicken stock or broth

Cinnamon, to taste
Nutmeg, to taste
Salt and pepper, to taste

1	cup heavy cream
1	cup Vermont maple syrup

Heat oil in a soup pot over medium heat. Add onion and garlic; cook, stirring often for 5 minutes. Add pumpkin and cook, stirring often, for 5 minutes. Add wine and simmer until reduced by half. Add vegetable and chicken stock; cook until reduced by half (at this point, pumpkin should be soft – if not, continue cooking until soft).

Purée soup in a food processor or blender (be careful – it will be very hot). Return soup to pot. Season with cinnamon, nutmeg, salt and pepper. Stir in cream and maple syrup. Reheat, if necessary, and serve.

Echo Lake Inn

Located five minutes from Okemo ski resort in Vermont's Central Lakes Region, the Echo Lake Inn was built in 1840 as a summer hotel. The inn's rich heritage includes frequent visits by President Calvin Coolidge, Henry Ford, Thomas Edison and other notable figures. Amenities include swimming, tennis, Jacuzzi and a dock on Echo Lake with canoes and row boats. Golf, hiking, biking and horseback riding are also close at hand.

The inn's restaurant, recently featured in both *Gourmet* and *Bon Appétit*, is well known for its excellent food and service.

INNKEEPERS:	Laurence Jeffery
ADDRESS:	Route 100 North
	Ludlow, Vermont 05149
TELEPHONE:	(802) 228-8602; (800) 356-6844
E-MAIL:	echolkinn@aol.com
WEBSITE:	www.echolakeinn.com
ROOMS:	23 Rooms; 7 Suites; Private baths
CHILDREN:	Welcome
ANIMALS:	Not allowed; Resident dog
HANDICAPPED:	Not handicapped accessible
DIETARY NEEDS:	Will accommodate guests' special dietary needs

Curried Vermont Apple Soup

Makes 4 Servings

"This recipe has been published in both Gourmet *and* Bon Appétit *magazine."*
~ Innkeeper, Echo Lake Inn

½	stick butter
1	medium onion, chopped
3	medium apples, peeled and sliced
1	tablespoon curry powder, plus extra for garnish
2	cups chicken stock or broth
1	cup heavy cream

Salt and pepper, to taste
Sour cream, for garnish (optional)

Melt butter in a large, heavy saucepan over medium heat. Add onions and cook until translucent. Add apples and cook until they start to soften. Stir in curry powder. Raise heat to medium-high and, while stirring, slowly add stock. Stir in cream. Bring to a boil, lower heat and simmer for 30 minutes, stirring occasionally. Season with salt, pepper and more curry powder, as needed. Dust rims of serving bowls with a little curry powder. Serve soup with a dollop of sour cream, if desired.

Strong House Inn

Built by Samuel Paddock Strong in 1834 and listed on the National Register of Historic Places, the Strong House Inn is ranked as one of the finest examples of early Greek Revival architecture in the area. Enjoy the ambiance of the enchanting English Garden Cottage. Or, celebrate a crimson sunset with the backdrop of the Adirondack Mountains.

The Adirondack Room is the ultimate romantic hideaway, reflecting the style of great turn-of-the-century Adirondack camps. The room features a magnificent canopied four-poster Adirondack bed and a floor-to-ceiling stone fireplace.

INNKEEPERS:	Mary & Hugh Bargiel
ADDRESS:	94 West Main Street
	Vergennes, Vermont 05491
TELEPHONE:	(802) 877-3337
E-MAIL:	innkeeper@stronghouseinn.com
WEBSITE:	www.stronghouseinn.com
ROOMS:	14 Rooms; Private baths
CHILDREN:	Children age 8 and older welcome
ANIMALS:	Not allowed; Resident cat
HANDICAPPED:	Handicapped accessible
DIETARY NEEDS:	Will accommodate guests' special dietary needs

Roasted Red Pepper Soup

Makes 4 to 6 Servings

4	large red bell peppers
4	cups chicken broth
2	cups seeded chopped tomatoes
1	cup diced potato
2	cloves garlic, minced
½	cup sour cream, room temperature

Salt and pepper, to taste

Roast bell peppers on a grill, over the flame on a gas stove or in a broiler until outside of pepper is well charred. Place peppers in a paper bag for a few minutes (this steams them and makes them easier to peel). Peel, seed and coarsely chop peppers.

Combine bell peppers, chicken broth, tomatoes, potatoes and garlic in a medium saucepan over medium-high heat. Bring to a boil, lower heat and simmer until potatoes are tender. Purée soup in a blender or food processor (be careful – the soup will be very hot). Return soup to saucepan. Stir in sour cream. Season with salt and pepper. Serve hot or cold.

The Inn at Stockbridge

Stockbridge is the heart of the Berkshires, a town described by Norman Rockwell as "the best of America, the best of New England." Steeped in history, celebrity, romance and intrigue, the town has a timeless appeal, with each season stamped with its own beauty and charm.

The Inn at Stockbridge, a Georgian-style mansion with large white pillars, was built as a private residence in 1906 and lovingly restored in 1982 as a bed & breakfast. Set back from the road on 12 secluded acres, the inn is just one mile from downtown Stockbridge.

INNKEEPERS:	Alice & Len Schiller
ADDRESS:	Route 7, Box 618
	Stockbridge, Massachusetts 01262
TELEPHONE:	(413) 298-3337; (888) 466-7865
E-MAIL:	innkeeper@stockbridgeinn.com
WEBSITE:	www.stockbridgeinn.com
ROOMS:	8 Rooms; 8 Suites; Private baths
CHILDREN:	Children age 12 and older welcome
ANIMALS:	Not allowed; Resident dog
HANDICAPPED:	Handicapped accessible
DIETARY NEEDS:	Will accommodate guests' special dietary needs

Easy Potato Leek Soup

Makes 8 to 12 Servings

½   stick butter or ¼ cup vegetable oil
3   cups diced leeks or yellow onion
4   medium Yukon Gold potatoes, peeled and diced
6   cups milk, water, chicken broth or a combination
2   teaspoons salt
White pepper, to taste
¼-½ cup heavy cream (optional)
2-4 tablespoons minced parsley, for garnish

Heat butter or oil in a large saucepan over medium heat. Add leeks or onions and toss to coat. Cook, covered, for about 10 minutes, until soft but not brown. Add potatoes, milk, water or broth and salt. Season with white pepper. Bring to a boil, lower heat and simmer, partially covered, for 30 minutes.

Strain soup; return strained liquid to saucepan and purée strained leek mixture. Add puréed leek mixture to saucepan. Bring to a simmer. Add more salt and white pepper, if needed. If soup is too thick, add more milk, water and/or broth. Just before serving, stir in cream, if desired. Garnish with parsley to serve.

The Wauwinet

Located just nine miles from bustling Nantucket Town and adjacent to the Great Point Wildlife Sanctuary, the Wauwinet is a serene retreat that combines the luxurious comfort of a wealthy friend's New England seaside estate with the sophistication of an elegant European inn.

Rated as one of North America's finest restaurants and a continual recipient of the Wine Spectator's "Grand Award" and Wine Enthusiast's "Award of Excellence," Topper's restaurant offers guests an extraordinary dining experience with gracious personalized service.

INNKEEPERS:	Eric & Bettina Landt
ADDRESS:	120 Wauwinet Road
	Nantucket, Massachusetts 02554
TELEPHONE:	(508) 228-0145; (800) 426-8718
E-MAIL:	wauwinet@relaischateaux.com
WEBSITE:	www.wauwinet.com
ROOMS:	26 Rooms; 7 Cottages; Private baths
CHILDREN:	Children age 18 and older welcome
ANIMALS:	Not allowed
HANDICAPPED:	Handicapped accessible
DIETARY NEEDS:	Will accommodate guests' special dietary needs

Wauwinet Lobster "Cobb" Salad

Makes 6 Servings

Citrus vinaigrette:
- ¾ cup grape seed oil
- 2 tablespoons lemon juice
- 2 tablespoons orange juice
- 1 tablespoon chopped chives
- 1 tablespoon minced shallots

Salt and pepper, to taste
Minced zest of 1 lemon

Salad:
- ½ pound pancetta, sliced ¼-inch-thick and diced into ¼-inch pieces
- 1 avocado, chopped into large dice
- ½ pound haricots vert (green beans), trimmed and blanched
- 9 baby artichokes, cooked and halved
- 1 pound assorted baby salad greens
- 3 (1½-pound) lobsters, cooked, meat removed
- 6 radishes, thinly sliced

Edible flowers, for garnish

For the vinaigrette: Whisk together all vinaigrette ingredients until thoroughly combined.

For the salad: Cook pancetta in a skillet over medium heat until crisp; set aside and keep warm. In a stainless steel bowl, toss avocado, green beans and artichokes with ½ cup of citrus vinaigrette. In a separate bowl, toss baby greens with enough vinaigrette to coat greens. Place an equal amount of baby greens in center of each of 6 plates.

In a bowl, toss lobster with remaining vinaigrette. Arrange lobster meat from ½ tail and 1 claw on each plate. Add green beans on plates, with beans coming through claw. Arrange avocado and 3 baby artichoke halves around lobster. Sprinkle with some pancetta and radishes. Drizzle a little vinaigrette over each salad, if desired. Garnish with edible flowers.

Harraseeket Inn

The two restaurants at the Harraseeket Inn use only the finest organic and natural Maine produce, wild seafood and game and make all their breads and desserts daily. Sample the award-winning cuisine in the Maine Dining Room. The atmosphere is refined yet cozy, warmed by two fireplaces. And, of course, Maine lobsters are always available.

Sunday brunch is not to be missed. It's an elegant array featuring a carving station, whole poached salmon, Belgian waffles with seasonal fruits and gourmet specialties such as caviar, pâtés, terrines and artisanal cheeses.

INNKEEPERS:	Nancy Gray
ADDRESS:	162 Main Street
	Freeport, Maine 04032
TELEPHONE:	(207) 865-9377; (800) 342-6432
E-MAIL:	harraseeke@aol.com
WEBSITE:	www.harraseeketinn.com
ROOMS:	84 Rooms; 2 Suites; 8 Cottages; Private baths
CHILDREN:	Children welcome
ANIMALS:	Small dogs allowed
HANDICAPPED:	Handicapped accessible
DIETARY NEEDS:	Will accommodate guests' special dietary needs

Turkey, Apple & Pecan Salad

Makes 4 Servings

2	cups cubed roasted turkey (leftover Thanksgiving turkey is ideal)
2	cups diced red or green apples (about 2 apples)
¼	cup thinly sliced celery
⅓	cup dried cherries
⅓	cup coarsely chopped pecans, toasted

Fresh salad greens

Dressing:

⅓	cup mayonnaise
⅓	cup sour cream
1	tablespoon lemon juice
1	tablespoon honey, warmed slightly (aids mixing)
½	teaspoon salt
¼	teaspoon pepper

Combine turkey, apples, celery, cherries and pecans. Add dressing to turkey mixture and toss to coat. Divide salad greens among 4 plates. Top green with turkey mixture and serve.

For the dressing: Combine all dressing ingredients.

Appetizers

Salmon Pâté 195

Elegant Artichoke Dip 197

Three Late Afternoon Dips 199

Corn & Wild Rice Cakes with Smoked Salmon 201

Crab & Shrimp Egg Toasts 203

Blue Harbor House Crab Cakes 205

Caramelized Onion & Goat Cheese Tart 207

Portobello Venezia 209

Stuffed Portobello Mushrooms with Sun-Dried Tomato Purée 211

Appetizers

Hill Farm Inn

Hill Farm Inn, one of Vermont's first bed & breakfast inns, specializes in warm country hospitality. This is the kind of place where there's always plenty to do, but never anything you have to do. And it's been this way for nearly 100 years. Set on 50 acres, with a mile of frontage on the famed Battenkill river, you'll enjoy spectacular mountain views in every direction.

The inn's convenient, but tucked away location between Manchester and Bennington provides easy access to a wide variety of cultural activities, shopping, dining, fishing, canoeing, hiking, skiing and fall foliage tours.

INNKEEPERS:	Lisa & Al Gray
ADDRESS:	458 Hill Farm Road
	Arlington, Vermont 05250
TELEPHONE:	(802) 375-2269; (800) 882-2545
E-MAIL:	stay@hillfarminn.com
WEBSITE:	www.hillfarminn.com
ROOMS:	5 Rooms; 6 Suites; 4 Cottages; Private baths
CHILDREN:	Children welcome
ANIMALS:	Not allowed; Resident goats, sheep, chickens, dog
HANDICAPPED:	Not handicapped accessible
DIETARY NEEDS:	Will accommodate guests' special dietary needs

Salmon Pâté

Makes 6 to 8 Servings

"This is a great appetizer that even non-fish eaters enjoy." ~ Innkeeper, Hill Farm Inn

1	(16-ounce) can red sockeye salmon, drained and flaked
1	(8-ounce) package cream cheese, softened
1	tablespoon lemon juice
1	tablespoon grated onion
2	teaspoons prepared horseradish
¼	teaspoon salt
¾	teaspoon Liquid Smoke
½	cup chopped pecans
2	tablespoons chopped fresh parsley

Cocktail rye bread or crackers, for serving

Combine all ingredients, except pecans and parsley, by hand. If mixture is very soft, refrigerate for a few minutes. Combine pecans and parsley. Form salmon mixture into a ball. Roll ball in pecan mixture. Chill for at least 3 hours. Serve with cocktail rye bread or crackers.

York Harbor Inn

The York Harbor Inn is an oceanfront bed & breakfast on the rocky coast of Maine. The inn offers luxurious accommodations in historic York Harbor. Many rooms feature Jacuzzi tubs, fireplaces, ocean views and a patio or deck. The inn features award-winning, gourmet, ocean-view dining with an emphasis on local seafood. The casual Ship's Cellar Pub is paneled with planking from early 19th century ships.

From the inn, you can walk to the beach and harbor, visit nearby lighthouses, play golf, shop at the Kittery Outlet stores and enjoy plenty of Maine lobster.

INNKEEPERS:	Garry Dominguez
ADDRESS:	Coastal Route 1A
	York Harbor, Maine 03911
TELEPHONE:	(207) 363-5119; (800) 343-3869
E-MAIL:	info@yorkharborinn.com
WEBSITE:	www.yorkharborinn.com
ROOMS:	46 Rooms; 1 Suite; Private baths
CHILDREN:	Welcome
ANIMALS:	Not allowed
HANDICAPPED:	Handicapped accessible
DIETARY NEEDS:	Will accommodate guests' special dietary needs

Elegant Artichoke Dip

Makes 6 to 8 Servings

"This dip can be made three days ahead of time and refrigerated until needed. Serve with warm French bread." ~ Innkeeper, York Harbor Inn

1½	(8-ounce) packages cream cheese, softened
2	tablespoons finely diced onion
2	tablespoons Chablis wine
1½	teaspoons Dijon mustard
¾	teaspoon salt
¾	teaspoon paprika
½	teaspoon minced garlic
½	teaspoon white pepper
1	tablespoon fresh lemon juice
1	(15-ounce) can artichoke hearts, drained and cut into large dice
¼	cup finely diced red bell pepper
½	cup breadcrumbs
2	tablespoons butter, melted

French bread, warmed, for serving

Preheat oven to 350°F. Combine cream cheese, onions, wine, mustard, salt, paprika, garlic, white pepper and lemon juice in a food processor; process until well mixed. Add artichoke hearts and bell peppers; pulse just to blend. Place artichoke mixture in a 1-quart casserole dish.

Combine breadcrumbs and butter; sprinkle over artichoke mixture. Bake for about 20 minutes, or until top is lightly browned and dip is bubbling around edges. Serve immediately with warm French bread.

1855 Marshall Slocum Guest House

The Marshall Slocum Guest House has been meticulously restored to reflect the charm and beauty of its Victorian heritage while offering today's comforts. The Newport mansions, harbor and beaches are only steps away from the inn. All rooms include fluffy down comforters, robes, Greenwich Bay Trading Company toiletries and a chocolate treat at night.

A three-course breakfast is served each morning. Entrées may include fluffy Belgian waffles with fresh strawberries, crêpes with asparagus, ham and cheddar cheese sauce or peaches and cream French toast.

INNKEEPERS:	Joan Wilson & Julie Wilson
ADDRESS:	29 Kay Street
	Newport, Rhode Island 02840
TELEPHONE:	(401) 841 5120; (800) 372 5120
E-MAIL:	info@marshallslocuminn.com
WEBSITE:	www.marshallslocuminn.com
ROOMS:	6 Rooms; Private baths
CHILDREN:	Children age 12 and older welcome
ANIMALS:	Not allowed
HANDICAPPED:	Not handicapped accessible
DIETARY NEEDS:	Will accommodate guests' special dietary needs

Three Late Afternoon Dips

Makes About 2 Cups Each

"Every afternoon we put out nibbles and wine and soft drinks for our guests to enjoy in the parlor in winter or on the back deck in summer. These three recipes are our guests' favorites." ~ Innkeeper, 1855 Marshall Slocum Guest House

Boursin cheese:
- 2 (8-ounce) packages cream cheese, softened
- 1 stick butter, softened
- 2 cloves garlic
- 1 teaspoon oregano
- ¼ teaspoon thyme
- ¼ teaspoon black pepper
- ¼ teaspoon dill
- ¼ teaspoon basil

Process all ingredients in a food processor until smooth.

Blue cheese pecan spread:
- 1⅓ cups pecans
- ½ cup crumbled blue cheese
- 1½ (8-ounce) packages cream cheese, softened

Process pecans in a food processor for 10 seconds. Add blue cheese and cream cheese; process for 30 seconds.

Hummus:
- 1 (19-ounce) can Goya chickpeas (garbanzo beans)
- ¼ cup tahini
- ½ cup olive oil
- ½ cup hot water
- Juice of 2 lemons
- ¾ teaspoon salt
- 1 teaspoon cumin
- Pepper, to taste

Process all ingredients in a food processor until smooth.

Beach Plum Inn

The Beach Plum Inn is located on seven acres, offering spectacular sea views, formal gardens and privacy for those who wish it. To while away the days, swim on beautiful private ocean beaches or enjoy croquet with a view on the inn's regulation court.

The inn's restaurant, ranked as the best on Martha's Vineyard and "top six in New England" by *Food & Wine* magazine, features award-winning cuisine served with spectacular views from every table. Culinary works of art are prepared from fresh, local seafood, aged beef and free-range chicken.

INNKEEPERS:	The Arnold Family
ADDRESS:	50 Beach Plum Lane
	Menemsha, Massachusetts 02552
TELEPHONE:	(508) 645-9454; (877) 645-7398
E-MAIL:	info@beachpluminn.com
WEBSITE:	www.beachpluminn.com
ROOMS:	11 Rooms; Private baths
CHILDREN:	Children welcome
ANIMALS:	Not allowed
HANDICAPPED:	Handicapped accessible
DIETARY NEEDS:	Will accommodate guests' special dietary needs

Corn & Wild Rice Cakes with Smoked Salmon

Makes 6 Servings

1¾	cups all-purpose flour
2	tablespoons sugar
2	teaspoons baking powder
½	teaspoon salt
3	eggs
1¼	cups buttermilk
½	stick butter, melted
½	cup cooked, drained wild rice
½	cup fresh corn (or frozen corn)
6	tablespoons crème fraîche
½	pound high quality Norwegian smoked salmon, thinly sliced

Sift flour, sugar, baking powder and salt into medium bowl. Add eggs, buttermilk and melted butter; beat until smooth and creamy. Fold in wild rice and corn.

Heat a skillet over medium heat until a few drops of water dance across the surface. Add batter to pan using about 2 tablespoons of batter per cake. Cook first side until bubbles form and edges look dry. Turn and cook until second side is a rich, golden brown. Serve immediately (can be made 1 day ahead, covered, refrigerated and reheated in a 350°F oven for 2-3 minutes).

Put 1 corn and wild rice cake in center of each plate. Coat each cake with 1 teaspoon of crème fraîche. Criss-cross 2 slices of smoked salmon over each cake. Repeat layers of 1 corn cake, 1 teaspoon of crème fraîche and 2 slices of smoked salmon 2 more times to yield a 3-layer-tall tower. Beautiful and delicious!

Primrose Inn

The Primrose Inn built in 1878 as a summer guest house, became the home of C.S. Leffingwell, the first pastor of St. Savior's Church. The home is one of Bar Harbor's last grand residences of the 19th century. It is a truly impressive interpretation of Victorian "Stick-Style" architecture, offering travelers a premiere lodging experience in the lovely coastal village of Bar Harbor, just one-half mile from Acadia National Park.

Guests of the inn enjoy a hearty breakfast, served fireside or, weather permitting, on the wraparound porch.

INNKEEPERS:	Pamela Parker & Bryan Stevens
ADDRESS:	73 Mount Desert Street
	Bar Harbor, Maine 04609
TELEPHONE:	(207) 288-4031; (877) 846-3424
E-MAIL:	relax@primroseinn.com
WEBSITE:	www.primroseinn.com
ROOMS:	11 Rooms; 4 Suites; Private baths
CHILDREN:	Children welcome in suites
ANIMALS:	Not allowed; Resident Westie
HANDICAPPED:	Not handicapped accessible
DIETARY NEEDS:	Cannot accommodate guests' special dietary needs

Crab & Shrimp Egg Toasts

Makes 4 Servings

1	(6½-ounce) can crabmeat (or use fresh crabmeat)
10-12	medium shrimp, cooked, peeled and chopped
1	(3-ounce) package cream cheese, cubed
2	ounces goat cheese, crumbled
9	hard-boiled eggs, peeled and chopped
2	tablespoons finely chopped chives or green onions
¼	cup mayonnaise
1-2	tablespoons Dijon mustard

Dash of salt
Dash of Old Bay seasoning (optional)
4   English muffins, split and toasted
Paprika, for garnish (optional)

Preheat broiler. In a medium bowl, combine crab, shrimp, cream cheese, goat cheese, eggs and chives; toss lightly to mix. In a small bowl, combine mayonnaise, mustard, salt and Old Bay seasoning; gently fold into crab mixture. Spoon crab mixture onto English muffin halves. Sprinkle with paprika. Broil about 6 inches from heat source until heated through.

Blue Harbor House

The Blue Harbor House is a classic New England Cape bed & breakfast built in 1810. Today, its historic charms blend perfectly with modern comforts. Relax in the parlor or in a rocker on the porch, or set off to explore Camden's harbor, shops and galleries. There's so much to do on your Maine coast vacation – "where the mountains meet the sea" – including boat trips, kayaking, hiking, swimming and antiquing.

Mornings start with delicious breakfast items such as cheese soufflés, potato quiches or blueberry pancakes with maple syrup and blueberry butter.

INNKEEPERS:	Jody Schmoll & Dennis Hayden
ADDRESS:	67 Elm Street
	Camden, Maine 04843
TELEPHONE:	(207) 236-3196; (800) 248-3196
E-MAIL:	balidog@blueharborhouse.com
WEBSITE:	www.blueharborhouse.com
ROOMS:	7 Rooms; 3 Suites; Private baths
CHILDREN:	Children age 12 and older welcome
ANIMALS:	Dogs & cats welcome; Resident dog
HANDICAPPED:	Not handicapped accessible
DIETARY NEEDS:	Will accommodate guests' special dietary needs

Blue Harbor House Crab Cakes

Makes 4 to 5 Servings

"Fresh peas are also delightful in these scrumptious crab cakes." – Innkeeper, Blue Heron House

1	tablespoon olive oil
¼	cup minced onion
2	cloves garlic, minced
¼	cup corn (optional)
2	tablespoons chopped celery
4	ounces shiitake mushrooms, chopped
¼	cup white wine

Seasoning salt, to taste*

¼	cup finely chopped parsley
6-10	ounces fresh crabmeat, picked over for shells
1	egg, beaten
¼	cup mayonnaise
1	tablespoon chopped fresh basil

Unseasoned dry or fresh breadcrumbs

1	tablespoons butter

Heat oil in a skillet over medium heat. Add onion, garlic, corn and celery; cook until onion is soft. Add mushrooms and wine; cook until liquids are absorbed. Add seasoning salt to taste, about 1 teaspoon. Remove from heat and cool.

Shred crabmeat into a bowl. Mix in egg, mayonnaise, basil and mushroom mixture. Mix in enough breadcrumbs so mixture holds together (mixture should be firm but not dry). Form into about ½-inch-thick patties. Melt butter in a skillet over medium-low heat. Add crab cakes and cook until golden brown on both sides. Serve hot.

*Note: To make your own seasoning salt, try a mixture of nutmeg, allspice, cinnamon, garlic salt, ground ginger, thyme, crushed red pepper flakes and a little cayenne pepper.

Gateways Inn

The Arthur Fiedler Suite at the Gateways Inn features a large sitting room and a spacious bedroom separated by French doors hung with Venetian lace curtains. Both rooms feature a working gas fireplace. The bathroom, with the original corner marble sink, Italian marble-tiled floor, large Jacuzzi tub and plush robes, offers a spa-like experience.

From the French Aubusson print bedding and the antique armoire in the bedroom to the plush, deep-green sofas and the Mahogany library with dry-bar, the suite is a subtly luxurious accommodation.

INNKEEPERS:	Fabrizio & Rosemary Chiariello
ADDRESS:	51 Walker Street
	Lenox, Massachusetts 01240
TELEPHONE:	(413) 637-2532; (888) 492-9466
E-MAIL:	gateways@berkshire.net
WEBSITE:	www.gatewaysinn.com
ROOMS:	11 Rooms; 1 Suite; Private baths
CHILDREN:	Children age 10 and older welcome
ANIMALS:	Not allowed
HANDICAPPED:	Not handicapped accessible
DIETARY NEEDS:	Will accommodate guests' special dietary needs

Caramelized Onion & Goat Cheese Tart

Makes 15 Small Tarts

Tarts:
Pie or unflavored pizza dough
Olive oil

Goat cheese spread:
1 (8-ounce) package goat cheese, softened
½ cup heavy cream
1 tablespoon lemon juice
Dash of salt and white pepper

Caramelized onions:
2 tablespoons olive oil
3 large yellow or Spanish onions, thinly sliced
1 clove garlic, minced
1 teaspoon salt
1 teaspoon pepper
1 teaspoon sugar
2 teaspoons finely chopped flat leaf parsley

For the tarts: Preheat oven to 350°F. On a floured surface, roll out pie or pizza dough ⅛-inch thick. Cut dough into 15 (4-inch) circles. Pierce dough randomly with a fork. Brush lightly with olive oil. Bake for 5-7 minutes, until golden brown and crisp. Remove from oven and cool.

For the goat cheese spread: Combine all spread ingredients.

For the caramelized onions: Heat olive oil in a large skillet over low heat. Add onions and cook until translucent. Add garlic, salt, pepper and sugar; cook for about 10-15 minutes, until onions are dark brown and sweet. Stir in parsley. Remove from heat and cool.

To assemble: Spread some goat cheese mixture over each crust. Spread caramelized onions over goat cheese. Bake for 5-7 minutes.

Beal House Inn

The circa 1833 Beal House Inn is a newly renovated gem that retains its original, Colonial Federal-style architecture. The inn received the 2003 Great American Main Street Award. Its popular, award-winning restaurant features "global cuisine without boundaries."

Perched under the eaves, atop a winding staircase on the third floor, the Notchway Suite is a large, two-bedroom suite, decorated in knotty pine and overlooking the woods at the back of the inn. The suite is your own private getaway with two entrances, the second featuring a private deck.

INNKEEPERS:	Catherine & Jose Luis Pawelek
ADDRESS:	2 West Main Street
	Littleton, New Hampshire 03561
TELEPHONE:	(603) 444-2661; (888) 616-2325
E-MAIL:	info@bealhouseinn.com
WEBSITE:	www.bealhouseinn.com
ROOMS:	3 Rooms; 5 Suites; Private baths
CHILDREN:	Children age 8 and older welcome
ANIMALS:	Small dogs allowed; Resident dogs
HANDICAPPED:	Handicapped accessible; Call ahead
DIETARY NEEDS:	Will accommodate guests' special dietary needs

Portobello Venezia

Makes 4 Servings

"It was very important to us to offer vegetarian entrées, so we created this dish. Through the years, it has become equally popular with our non-vegetarian guests!" ~ Innkeeper, Beal House Inn

1	teaspoon olive oil
1	cup trimmed fresh spinach
4	large portobello mushrooms, stems removed
½	cup demi-glace (¼ cup of concentrated demi-glace mixed with ¼ cup water)*
½	cup red wine
5	sprigs fresh rosemary, divided
1	cup sliced mushrooms (mix of white, porcini, crimini, etc.)
4	slices prosciutto (optional)
4	slices Provolone or Mozzarella cheese
2	cups mashed potatoes, warmed

Preheat grill. Heat oil in a small skillet over medium heat. Add spinach and cook until done; set aside and keep warm. Grill portobello mushrooms on each side for 2 minutes (or use a skillet with a touch of vegetable oil).

Preheat oven to 375°F. Combine demi-glace, wine, 1 sprig of rosemary and sliced mushrooms in a large, oven-proof skillet; bring to a boil, lower heat and simmer for 4-5 minutes, until sauce is reduced to ½ cup. Put portobello mushrooms in skillet on top of sauce. Top each portobello mushroom with a slice of prosciutto and a slice of cheese. Transfer skillet to oven and bake for 2-3 minutes, or until cheese starts to melt.

Place a mound of mashed potatoes on each plate. Top with some spinach. Invert 1 portobello mushroom cap on top of spinach. Top with some pan sauce. Garnish with a rosemary sprig to serve.

*Note: Concentrated demi-glace is a stock base that is available in many groceries and specialty food stores.

The Flying Cloud

Guest rooms at the Flying Cloud are named for the more legendary ports-of-call of the clipper ship, the Flying Cloud. Four rooms have beautiful water views of the tidal Damariscotta River and harbor. Take your first cup of morning coffee out onto the front deck and bask in the morning sun while you watch the lobster and pleasure boats in the busy harbor on the Damariscotta River.

Local activities include visiting Pemaquid Point Lighthouse and Beach, kayak tours, puffin cruises and whale watching and sunset sails.

INNKEEPERS:	Dave & Karen Bragg
ADDRESS:	45 River Road
	Newcastle, Maine 04553
TELEPHONE:	(207) 563-2484
E-MAIL:	stay@theflyingcloud.com
WEBSITE:	www.theflyingcloud.com
ROOMS:	5 Rooms; 1 Suite; Private baths
CHILDREN:	Children age 10 and older welcome
ANIMALS:	Not allowed
HANDICAPPED:	Not handicapped accessible
DIETARY NEEDS:	Will accommodate guests' special dietary needs

Stuffed Portobello Mushrooms with Sun-Dried Tomato Purée

Makes 6 Servings

Sun-dried tomato purée:
- ¼ cup sun-dried tomatoes (not oil-packed)
- 1 small clove garlic, chopped
- ½ cup plain yogurt

Stuffed portobello mushrooms:
- 2 cloves garlic, minced
- ½ cup olive oil
- 2 tablespoons light soy sauce
- 6 large portobello mushroom caps, cleaned well with a brush
- 1 tablespoon butter
- 9 large eggs
- 2½ tablespoons half & half
- ½ cup ricotta cheese
- 2 tablespoons chopped fresh herbs (tarragon and parsley are good)

For the sun-dried tomato purée: Put sun-dried tomatoes in 1 cup of boiling water until softened. Drain; discard water. Purée sun-dried tomatoes, garlic and yogurt in a food processor (if making ahead, cover and refrigerate).

For the mushrooms: Combine garlic, olive oil and soy sauce; generously brush on both sides of mushroom caps. Spray grill (or broiler pan) with non-stick cooking spray; grill or broil mushroom caps for about 3 minutes per side, until tender (if making ahead, cool, cover and set aside).

To serve: Melt butter in a large skillet over medium-high heat. Beat eggs and half & half; add to skillet and cook, stirring, until eggs are soft but still glossy. Dot eggs with ricotta cheese. Cook until cheese softens. Place a mushroom on each plate (if mushrooms were made ahead, reheat in a 300°F oven for 3-4 minutes). Top with eggs and sprinkle with fresh herbs. Serve with room temperature or warm sun-dried tomato purée on the side.

Note: The sun-dried tomato purée is best made a day ahead, covered and refrigerated to let the flavors marry.

Luncheon & Dinner Entrées

Scallop-Stuffed Salmon en Papillote 215

Smoked Salmon Ravioli 217

Pan-Seared Scallops with Capers & Lemon 219

Caramelized Nantucket Bay Scallops with Cucumbers, Upland Cress & Sesame Vinaigrette..221

Lobster Sauté 223

Mediterranean Shrimp 225

Calamari Alla Franco 227

Vermont Baked Veal..229

Autumn Brisket 231

Lobster Stuffed Chicken with Boursin Cheese Sauce 233

Luncheon & Dinner Entrées

Echo Lake Inn

Located in Vermont's beautiful central lakes region, the Echo Lake Inn was built in 1840 as a Victorian summer hotel. Today it remains one of the few authentic country inns operating year-round in Vermont.

"Dinner here is something of an event, cheerfully served under exposed beams on plum-colored linens, and accompanied by an affordable wine list. On weekends, so many people from Ludlow and other local communities dine here that two sittings are scheduled – a first-time visitor quickly understands why." ~ *Vermont Magazine*

INNKEEPERS:	Laurence Jeffery
ADDRESS:	Route 100 North
	Ludlow, Vermont 05149
TELEPHONE:	(802) 228-8602; (800) 356-6844
E-MAIL:	echolkinn@aol.com
WEBSITE:	www.echolakeinn.com
ROOMS:	23 Rooms; 7 Suites; Private baths
CHILDREN:	Welcome
ANIMALS:	Not allowed; Resident dog
HANDICAPPED:	Not handicapped accessible
DIETARY NEEDS:	Will accommodate guests' special dietary needs

Scallop-Stuffed Salmon en Papillote

Makes 4 Servings

"An elegant, but not difficult or time-consuming entrée. The secret to this dish is to fold the parchment paper tightly to seal in the flavors. Even though the salmon is baked, it is actually steamed in the paper." ~ Innkeeper, Echo Lake Inn

4	(8-ounce) boneless salmon filets
½	pound sea scallops
4	(12x16-inch) sheets parchment paper

Salt and pepper, to taste

1	lemon, thinly sliced
1	carrot, peeled and julienned
1	onion, peeled and julienned
1	rib celery, julienned
4	sprigs fresh dill
½	cup white wine
1	stick butter, cut into thin slices

Preheat oven to 425°F. Slice salmon lengthwise down center, about ¾ of the way through. Insert 3-4 scallops in each salmon filet. Center each salmon filet on ½ of a sheet of parchment paper.

Season salmon with salt and pepper. Top salmon with a couple of lemon slices and some carrots, onions and celery. Top vegetables with a sprig of dill, a sprinkle of wine and a few slices of butter.

Fold parchment paper tightly over salmon. Crimp edges by making overlapping folds every inch or so. Bake for 15 minutes. Serve salmon sealed in parchment – let your guests open these delicious packages!

The 1785 Inn

The dining room at the 1785 Inn is renowned for its outstanding cuisine and service. Candlelight casts a romantic glow throughout the evening, inviting you to take your time and enjoy the pleasures of your meal. The restaurants wine list has been awarded *Wine Spectator's* "Award of Excellence" each year since 1986.

The 1785 Inn is convenient to North Conway and all the White Mountain attractions. The inn's cross-country ski trails offer interesting nature walks and fishing during the spring, summer and fall seasons.

INNKEEPERS:	Becky & Charlie Mallar
ADDRESS:	3582 White Mountain Highway
	North Conway, New Hampshire 03860
TELEPHONE:	(603) 356-9025; (800) 421-1785
E-MAIL:	the1785inn@aol.com
WEBSITE:	www.the1785inn.com
ROOMS:	17 Rooms; 1 Suite; Private & shared baths
CHILDREN:	Welcome
ANIMALS:	Not allowed
HANDICAPPED:	Not handicapped accessible
DIETARY NEEDS:	Will accommodate guests' special dietary needs

Smoked Salmon Ravioli

Makes 6 to 8 Servings

Pasta:
- 2 cups all-purpose flour
- 2 large eggs, beaten
- 2 egg yolks, beaten

Egg wash (1 egg beaten with 1 tablespoon of water)

Smoked salmon mousse:
- 1 pound smoked salmon filet
- 2 eggs
- 1 cup whipping cream, chilled
- ½ teaspoon coarsely ground pepper
- 2 tablespoons chopped chives

For serving:
- 2 cups grated Gruyère cheese
- 1 cup heavy cream

For the pasta: Put flour in a mound on a smooth work surface. Make a well in center of flour. Put eggs and egg yolks into well; slowly pull flour into eggs until well incorporated. Knead dough (add more flour if needed, for a smooth consistency). Divide dough in half and roll out each half or feed through a pasta machine until thin (number 6 setting on a pasta machine).

For the mousse: In a food processor, purée smoked salmon and eggs until smooth. Slowly add cream, pepper and chives; process until smooth.

Lay pasta on a floured surface. Place 24 mounds of mousse 2-inches apart on 1 sheet of pasta. Brush pasta with egg wash between mounds of mousse. Cover with second sheet of pasta. Press pasta to seal. Cut raviolis apart and refrigerate or freeze until ready to use.

To serve: Preheat broiler. Bring a large pot of lightly salted water to a boil. Add raviolis to water and cook for about 6 minutes. Sprinkle 2 tablespoons of cheese and 2 tablespoons of cream over each of 6-8 oven-proof plates. Broil until cheese melts. Put 3-4 ravioli on each plate and sprinkle with 2 tablespoons of cheese. Broil until cheese browns lightly.

The Blue Hill Inn

The Blue Hill Inn is an intimate bed & breakfast located in the sea coast village of Blue Hill. The inn, which has been hosting guests since 1840, is close to Castine, Brooklin, Sedgwick, Deer Isle and Stonington, and is a 45 minute drive from Acadia National Park and Bar Harbor.

"Blue Hill is the kind of coastal village – scenic and secluded, yet with fine cuisine and culture to spare – that travelers dream of finding when they come to Maine. And the Blue Hill Inn is the kind of classic New England hostelry they hope to discover once they arrive." ~ *Downeast Magazine*

INNKEEPERS:	Mary & Don Hartley
ADDRESS:	40 Union Street
	Blue Hill, Maine 04614
TELEPHONE:	(207) 374-2844; (800) 826-7415
E-MAIL:	mary@bluehillinn.com
WEBSITE:	www.bluehillinn.com
ROOMS:	10 Rooms; 2 Suites; Private baths
CHILDREN:	Welcome
ANIMALS:	Not allowed
HANDICAPPED:	Handicapped accessible
DIETARY NEEDS:	Will accommodate guests' special dietary needs

Pan-Seared Scallops with Capers & Lemon

Makes 4 Servings

"The tricks for producing tender scallops are to pat the scallops dry after rinsing and to cook them briefly in an uncrowded pan. Be sure to look for fresh, clean-smelling scallops that do not have water added. Larger sea scallops, not small bay scallop, should be used." - Innkeeper The Blue Hill Inn

1½	pounds dry packed sea scallops, muscles removed, rinsed sparingly and patted dry
4-6	tablespoons unsalted butter, divided
2	tablespoons minced shallots
⅓	cup capers, drained and dried, plus extra for garnish

Juice of 2 large lemons

Preheat plates. Heat a large skillet over medium-high heat. Cooking largest scallops first, place scallops in skillet, being careful not to crowd them (or they will steam). Sear scallops on one side, turn and sear the second side, cooking for 3-5 minutes (scallops are done when centers are translucent when looked at from the side); remove to warmed plates.

Melt 2 tablespoons of butter in a small saucepan over low heat. Add shallots and cook until translucent (be careful not to brown butter). Add lemon juice and reduce by half. Whisk in remaining butter, 1 tablespoon at a time. Pour sauce around scallops. Garnish with capers and serve immediately.

The Wauwinet

Experience the Wauwinet, Nantucket's premier resort. An idyllic blend of superior food, extraordinary service, gracious comfort and delightful surroundings has earned the Wauwinet critical acclaim, including membership in the prestigious association of Relais & Châteaux.

The inn's spectacular location provides an unmatched vantage point from which to explore Nantucket or, simply relax and enjoy the serenity of this peaceful island retreat. You will find all the amenities of a world-class retreat, combined with the charm and sophistication of a European inn.

INNKEEPERS:	Eric & Bettina Landt
ADDRESS:	120 Wauwinet Road
	Nantucket, Massachusetts 02554
TELEPHONE:	(508) 228-0145; (800) 426-8718
E-MAIL:	wauwinet@relaischateaux.com
WEBSITE:	www.wauwinet.com
ROOMS:	26 Rooms; 7 Cottages; Private baths
CHILDREN:	Children age 18 and older welcome
ANIMALS:	Not allowed
HANDICAPPED:	Handicapped accessible
DIETARY NEEDS:	Will accommodate guests' special dietary needs

Caramelized Nantucket Bay Scallops with Upland Cress, Cucumbers & Sesame Vinaigrette

Makes 6 Servings

Sesame vinaigrette:
- ½ cup rice wine vinegar
- ¼ cup lime juice
- 2 tablespoons sesame oil
- 2 teaspoons minced orange zest
- 1 tablespoon chopped chives
- ½ teaspoon crushed red pepper flakes
- Dash of Tabasco
- Freshly cracked black pepper, to taste

Caramelized scallops:
- 3 cucumbers
- ½ pound upland cress or watercress, washed
- 12 radishes, thinly sliced
- 2 teaspoons black sesame seeds, toasted
- 1 tablespoon extra-virgin olive oil
- 36 Nantucket bay scallops

For the vinaigrette: Combine all vinaigrette ingredients and let stand for 30 minutes to let flavors marry.

For the scallops: Peel cucumbers, then peel cucumber flesh with a vegetable peeler to make long strips, peeling until reaching seeds. Add cucumber strips to vinaigrette; toss to coat. Put some cucumbers in center of each plate. Arrange upland cress in 3 bunches around cucumber. Sprinkle radish slices over cress. Garnish with sesame seeds. Drizzle vinaigrette around plate.

Add olive oil to a very hot skillet. Add scallops and cook for no more than 1 minute, tossing frequently. Arrange scallops around salad to serve.

Harraseeket Inn

The AAA Four-Diamond Harraseeket Inn offers Maine's best vacation packages – from the "State of Mainer" to the inn's most popular Freeport vacation, "The Serious Shopper." The inn is just two blocks from L.L. Bean and over 170 other great stores. Discover why *Conde Nast Traveler* magazine rated the Harraseeket Inn as "One of the Top 500 Places to Stay in the World."

The Honeymoon Package includes a bottle of champagne on ice awaiting your arrival and a room service breakfast with champagne and strawberries.

INNKEEPERS:	Nancy Gray
ADDRESS:	162 Main Street
	Freeport, Maine 04032
TELEPHONE:	(207) 865-9377; (800) 342-6432
E-MAIL:	harraseeke@aol.com
WEBSITE:	www.harraseeketinn.com
ROOMS:	84 Rooms; 2 Suites; 8 Cottages; Private baths
CHILDREN:	Children welcome
ANIMALS:	Small dogs allowed
HANDICAPPED:	Handicapped accessible
DIETARY NEEDS:	Will accommodate guests' special dietary needs

Lobster Sauté

Makes 1 Serving

1	tablespoon butter
½	cup sliced leeks, divided
¼	cup sherry
2	cups heavy cream

Lobster spiders*
3	Maine Red Bliss baby potatoes, steamed and cooled
1	red bell pepper, roasted, peeled and sliced
½	ear Maine corn, roasted and kernels cut from cob
1	(1¼-pound) Maine lobster, steamed and cooled (meat picked from tail and claws)

Salt and pepper, to taste
Sliced chives, for garnish

Melt butter in a heavy-bottomed saucepan over medium heat. Add ¼ cup of leeks and cook lightly. Add sherry and bring to boil. Lower heat and add cream and lobster spiders. Simmer until reduced by half, then strain and keep warm.

Combine remaining ¼ cup of leeks, potatoes, bell pepper and corn in a skillet over medium heat. Add cream mixture and lobster meat. Season with salt and pepper. Cook until heated through. Garnished with chives to serve.

*Note: Lobster spiders are the body of a lobster with the legs intact and the claws and tail removed.

Stone Hill Inn

A scenic mountain village awaits guests at the doorstep of the Stone Hill Inn, a place for couples who treasure their time together. Stowe, with its New England charm, hints of European influence and natural beauty, has been welcoming visitors for two centuries.

"The Stone Hill Inn combines a coveted hilltop setting in the woods, tranquility, top-drawer construction, designer decor, gourmet breakfasts and gorgeous spacious private baths. It's an intimate place with only nine guest room – picture perfect." ~ Montreal Gazette

INNKEEPERS:	Amy & Hap Jordan
ADDRESS:	89 Houston Farm Road
	Stowe, Vermont 05672
TELEPHONE:	(802) 253-6282
E-MAIL:	stay@stonehillinn.com
WEBSITE:	www.stonehillinn.com
ROOMS:	9 Rooms; Private baths
CHILDREN:	Children age 18 and older welcome
ANIMALS:	Not allowed
HANDICAPPED:	Not handicapped accessible
DIETARY NEEDS:	Will accommodate guests' special dietary needs

Mediterranean Shrimp

Makes 12 Servings

"You will need wooden skewers for grilling or broiling these delicious shrimp."
~ Innkeeper, Stone Hill Inn

1½	cups olive oil
½	cup chopped fresh parsley
1½	tablespoons dried basil
1	tablespoon dried oregano
12	cloves garlic, minced
1½	tablespoons salt
2	tablespoons pepper
¼	cup fresh lemon juice
2	pounds raw shrimp, peeled (thawed, if frozen)

Lemon wedges, for serving

Combine all ingredients, except shrimp and lemon wedges. Put shrimp in a glass baking dish or other non-reactive container. Pour ⅔ of marinade over shrimp; stir well to coat. Cover and refrigerate shrimp for at least 1 hour. Reserve remaining ⅓ of marinade for grilling. Soak wooden skewers in water for at least 1 hour.

Preheat grill or broiler. Remove shrimp from marinade; discard marinade. Skewer shrimp and grill or broil, basting with reserved marinade, for 3 minutes per side, or until done. Serve with lemon wedges.

Casa Bella Inn

The Casa Bella Inn & Restaurant offers "a little bit of Tuscany" in a Vermont country inn. Recent restorations have created modern accommodations while retaining the inn's original grandeur. The inn's setting, architecture, casual, relaxed atmosphere and wonderful food combine to create an unforgettable experience.

Gaze at the mountains and forests and consider them your playground – Casa Bella Inn is just eight miles from Killington Ski Resort. Enjoy a full breakfast, afternoon refreshments and dinner in the inn's Italian restaurant.

INNKEEPERS:	Susan & Franco Cacozza
ADDRESS:	3911 Main Street Route 100
	Pittsfield, Vermont 05762
TELEPHONE:	(802) 746-8943; (877) 746-8943
E-MAIL:	info@casabellainn.com
WEBSITE:	www.casabellainn.com
ROOMS:	7 Rooms; 1 Suite; Private baths
CHILDREN:	Children age 10 and older welcome
ANIMALS:	Not allowed
HANDICAPPED:	Not handicapped accessible
DIETARY NEEDS:	Will accommodate guests' special dietary needs

Calamari Alla Franco

Makes 4 Servings

"Shrimp may be substituted for calamari." ~ Innkeeper, Casa Bella Inn

1	tablespoon olive oil
1	tablespoon minced garlic
12	squid tubes, cleaned, washed and sliced into rings
1	tablespoon capers
½	cup pitted Italian black olives
Pinch of dried oregano, plus dried or minced fresh oregano, for serving
Pinch of crushed red pepper flakes (optional)
Salt and pepper, to taste
2	cups tomato sauce

Heat oil in a skillet over medium heat. Add garlic and cook just until golden. Add calamari and cook for about 2 minutes, until opaque. Raise heat to medium-high and add capers and black olives; cook for 1 minute. Stir in oregano, red pepper flakes, salt and pepper. Add tomato sauce and cook for about 30 seconds, or until tomato sauce is hot and calamari is white and no longer transparent (be careful not to overcook). Serve immediately sprinkled with a little fresh or dried oregano.

The Vermont Inn

The Vermont Inn is a small, circa 1840 country inn on five acres in the Green Mountains. The inn combines the charm of a family-run bed & breakfast with excellent New England and Continental cuisine. Guests enjoy year-round outdoor adventures, with exceptional skiing in winter and myriad summer and fall activities in the surrounding mountains.

The highlight of the Vermont Inn is the fabulous, award-winning, gourmet cuisine. Guests of the inn are served a four-course dinner by a roaring fire in the huge field stone fireplace, accompanied by beautiful mountain views.

INNKEEPERS:	Megan & Greg Smith
ADDRESS:	Route 4
	Killington, Vermont 05751
TELEPHONE:	(802) 775-0708; (800) 541-7795
E-MAIL:	relax@vermontinn.com
WEBSITE:	www.vermontinn.com
ROOMS:	18 Rooms; 5 Suites; Private baths
CHILDREN:	Children age 6 and older welcome
ANIMALS:	Not allowed; Resident cats
HANDICAPPED:	Handicapped accessible
DIETARY NEEDS:	Will accommodate guests' special dietary needs

Vermont Baked Veal

Makes 4 Servings

1	pound veal top round
2	tablespoons olive oil
2	cloves garlic, minced
½	cup chopped shallots
1	cup chopped spinach
½	cup diced cooked bacon
2	cups grated cheddar cheese

Salt and pepper, to taste
Nutmeg, to taste

½	cup all-purpose flour
4	large eggs, slightly beaten
½	cup breadcrumbs

Preheat oven to 350°F. Cut veal into ¼-inch-thick slices and pound lightly until very thin; set aside. Heat oil in a skillet over medium heat. Add garlic, shallots and spinach; cook until shallots are soft, then remove from heat. Add bacon, cheese, salt, pepper and nutmeg to spinach mixture; stir until well combined.

Place ¼ cup of spinach mixture in center of each slice of veal; roll up tightly. Secure with toothpicks, if desired. Dredge veal rolls in flour, dip in egg and then roll in breadcrumbs. Put veal rolls on a greased baking sheet. Bake for 15-20 minutes, or until golden brown and cooked through.

Deer Brook Inn

Welcome to beautiful Woodstock and the Green Mountains. Enjoy a historic haven of hospitality and comfort surrounded by spacious lawns and gardens. Whether your vision of the idyllic New England bed & breakfast experience is replete with culture and recreation, or it involves simply sinking into a comfortable chair with a summer breeze or winter fire, the Deer Brook Inn sets the scene while allowing you to set the pace.

Enjoy a room filled with antique furnishings, original artwork and wide, honey pine floors. Then start your day with a full, candlelit breakfast.

INNKEEPERS:	David Kanal & George DeFina
ADDRESS:	535 Woodstock Road
	Woodstock, Vermont 05091
TELEPHONE:	(802) 672-3713
E-MAIL:	info@deerbrookinn.com
WEBSITE:	www.deerbrookinn.com
ROOMS:	4 Rooms; 1 Suite; Private baths
CHILDREN:	Welcome
ANIMALS:	Not allowed
HANDICAPPED:	Not handicapped accessible
DIETARY NEEDS:	Will accommodate guests' special dietary needs

Autumn Brisket

Makes 8 Servings

"This brisket is easy to make and is great comfort food for those cool days. It tastes even better reheated on the second day." ~ Innkeeper, Deer Brook Inn

½	cup vegetable oil, divided
3	large onions, sliced into 1-inch-thick slices
2	cloves garlic, chopped
1	(6-pound) beef brisket
1	cup packed dark brown sugar
¾	cup apple cider
1¼	cups ketchup
¼	cup water

Heat ¼ cup of oil in a large Dutch oven over medium heat. Add onions and garlic; cook until onions are lightly browned. Remove onions and garlic and set aside.

Heat remaining ¼ of oil in Dutch oven over high heat. Add brisket and sear on both sides. Lower heat to low. Top brisket with onion mixture. Combine brown sugar, apple cider, ketchup and water; pour over brisket. Cover and cook for 2½ hours. Uncover Dutch oven and cook for 1 hour longer, or until meat is fork-tender.

Note: This brisket can be made a 1-2 days in advance, covered, refrigerated and then reheated – it's often best served this way!

York Harbor Inn

The York Harbor Inn is an oceanfront bed & breakfast on the rocky coast of Maine. The inn offers luxurious accommodations in historic York Harbor. Many rooms feature Jacuzzi tubs, fireplaces, ocean views and a patio or deck. The inn features award-winning, gourmet, ocean-view dining with an emphasis on local seafood. The casual Ship's Cellar Pub is paneled with planking from early 19th century ships.

From the inn, you can walk to the beach and harbor, visit nearby lighthouses, play golf, shop at the Kittery Outlet stores and enjoy plenty of Maine lobster.

INNKEEPERS:	Garry Dominguez
ADDRESS:	Coastal Route 1A
	York Harbor, Maine 03911
TELEPHONE:	(207) 363-5119; (800) 343-3869
E-MAIL:	info@yorkharborinn.com
WEBSITE:	www.yorkharborinn.com
ROOMS:	46 Rooms; 1 Suite; Private baths
CHILDREN:	Welcome
ANIMALS:	Not allowed
HANDICAPPED:	Handicapped accessible
DIETARY NEEDS:	Will accommodate guests' special dietary needs

Lobster-Stuffed Chicken with Boursin Cheese Sauce

Makes 8 Servings

Stuffing:

- 2 tablespoons clarified butter
- 2 ounces onion, finely diced
- 2 ounces celery, finely diced
- 2 tablespoons dry sherry wine
- 1½ teaspoons minced garlic
- 1½ teaspoons Worcestershire sauce
- 10 ounces Ritz crackers, crushed
- 1 tablespoon sliced green onion
- 1 tablespoon chopped parsley
- 1 teaspoon salt
- 1 teaspoon white pepper

Chicken:

- 1 pound cooked lobster meat, cut into medium dice and divided
- 8 (6-ounce) boneless, skinless chicken breasts, lightly pounded
- 2 cups heavy cream
- 10 ounces garlic and herb Boursin cheese

For the stuffing: Heat butter in a skillet over medium heat. Add onion and celery and cook until limp. Transfer to a bowl. Add remaining stuffing ingredients and thoroughly combine.

For the chicken: Preheat oven to 350°F. Place ⅛ of stuffing and ⅛ of lobster in center of each chicken breast. Fold in sides of chicken and secure with toothpicks. Bring cream to a boil in a 2-quart saucepan. Whisk in Boursin cheese. Lower heat to low and cook very gently, scraping bottom of pan with a rubber spatula often, so cheese does not burn. Cook until sauce is lightly thickened (sauce may be held for a short time in warm water bath). Bake chicken for about 18 minutes, until done. Top chicken with Boursin cheese mixture to serve.

Fruit Specialties

Pears in Mascarpone Custard 237

Strawberry Peach Compote in Sweet Wine Syrup......................239

Drunken Bananas 241

Strawberries Romanoff 243

Baked Peaches with Raspberries & Cream 245

Bohemian Plum Dumplings 247

Claddagh Cranberry Conserve & Chutney................................249

Mango Smoothie 251

Fresh Blueberry Pie..253

Sour Cream Rhubarb Streusel Pie..255

Catherine's Tarte Tatin 257

Plum Torte 259

Nantucket Cranberry Apple Crisp 261

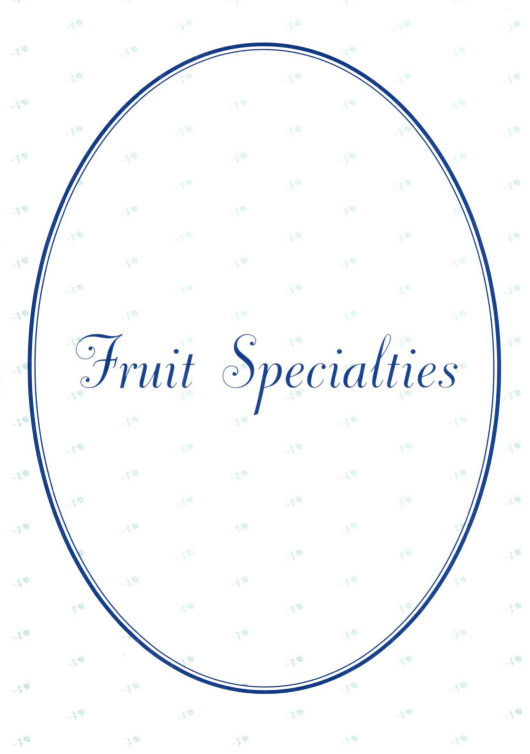

Fruit Specialties

The Crowes' Nest

No matter what the season, the Crowes' Nest combines the amenities of Jackson Village with the peace and serenity of Thorn Mountain. From the Crowes' Nest, enjoy breathtaking sunsets overlooking the White Mountains. Take long peaceful walks through White Mountain National Forest, explore Jackson Falls or play a round of golf.

Rooms offer guests an experience of understated elegance. Peter's Room, located in the Lodge, has a king-size bed, private bath, fireplace, Jacuzzi tub, private balcony and Continental decor.

INNKEEPERS:	Christine & Myles Crowe
ADDRESS:	Ten Evergreen Trail
	Jackson, New Hampshire 03846
TELEPHONE:	(603) 383-8913; (800) 511-8383
E-MAIL:	tcnest@crowesnest.net
WEBSITE:	www.crowesnest.net
ROOMS:	7 Rooms; Private baths
CHILDREN:	Welcome (no cribs provided)
ANIMALS:	Not allowed
HANDICAPPED:	Not handicapped accessible
DIETARY NEEDS:	Will accommodate guests' special dietary needs

Pears in Mascarpone Custard

Makes 6 Servings

3	medium pears, peeled and diced
2	tablespoons Scotch liquor (optional)
1	tablespoon plus ½ cup sugar
½	stick butter or margarine
1	egg
⅔	cup mascarpone cheese
2	tablespoons all-purpose flour

Fresh mint sprigs, for garnish

Preheat oven to 350°F. Divide pears among 6 buttered 6- or 8-ounce ramekins. Sprinkle pears with liquor, if desired, and 1 tablespoon of sugar.

In a bowl, cream together butter and ½ cup of sugar. Beat in egg, then beat in mascarpone cheese. Add flour and mix well. Spoon butter mixture over pears. Bake for 50 minutes, until topping is just set. Garnish with mint sprigs to serve.

1831 Zachariah Eddy House

Specializing in unique getaway packages, the 1831 Zachariah Eddy House Bed & Breakfast offers over 50 different getaways throughout the year. Arrington's Bed & Breakfast Journal recognized the inn nationally for "Best Getaway Packages" in its 2003 Book of Lists.

The Chapel Bath was built by the home's original owners as a chapel in the late 1800s. It was sensitively restored as a bath by the current innkeepers. The highlight of the room is a magnificent Oriel stained glass window, no doubt a museum piece, which dazzles brilliantly in the early morning sun.

INNKEEPERS:	Bradford & Cheryl Leonard
ADDRESS:	51 South Main Street
	Middleboro, Massachusetts 02346
TELEPHONE:	(508) 946-0016
E-MAIL:	info@1831eddyhousebb.com
WEBSITE:	www.1831eddyhousebb.com
ROOMS:	3 Rooms; Private & shared baths
CHILDREN:	Children welcome; call ahead
ANIMALS:	Not allowed
HANDICAPPED:	Not handicapped accessible
DIETARY NEEDS:	Will accommodate guests' special dietary needs

Strawberry Peach Compote in Sweet Wine Syrup

Makes 6 Servings

"This is served as the fruit course on sizzling summer mornings. It is simple, but elegant and always a favorite." ~ Innkeeper, 1831 Zachariah Eddy House Bed & Breakfast

2	cups peach Chardonnay wine
6	tablespoons sugar
1	tablespoon Amaretto liqueur
¼	cup fresh blueberries (optional)
3	fresh peaches, washed and thinly sliced
1	pint strawberries, rinsed, dried, hulled and thinly sliced
6	scoops frozen peach yogurt or ice cream
1	(15-ounce) can whipped cream
6	sprigs fresh mint, for garnish

In a 1-quart jar, combine peach Chardonnay, sugar and Amaretto. Cover tightly and shake well to mix. Chill for 1 hour.

Put a few blueberries, if desired, in each of 6 pieces of crystal stemware, large wine glasses or other nice serving glasses or dishes. Layer peaches and strawberries in stemware until about ⅔-full (reserve some peach and strawberry slices for garnish). If using blueberries, sprinkle very lightly throughout, just to add a little extra color.

Pour Chardonnay mixture over fruit. Just before serving, add a scoop of frozen yogurt to each glass. Finish with a generous swirl of whipped cream. Garnish with a sprig of fresh mint and a peach and/or strawberry slice.

Sinclair Inn

West of the Green Mountains and east of Lake Champlain, the Sinclair Inn invites guests to step back in time to a bygone era. Located just 15 miles from Burlington, this historic, fully restored, circa 1890 Victorian inn features original crown moldings, fret work, hardwood floors and stained glass windows.

On cold days, the living room's fireplace beckons guests to relax and curl up with a good book. In summer, stroll past the stone pond and cascading waterfall to the back of the gardens which overlook the Green Mountains.

INNKEEPERS:	Sally & Bruce Gilbert-Smith
ADDRESS:	389 Vermont Route 15
	Jericho, Vermont 05465
TELEPHONE:	(802) 899-2234; (800) 433-4658
E-MAIL:	innkeeper@sinclairinnbb.com
WEBSITE:	www.sinclairinnbb.com
ROOMS:	6 Rooms; Private baths
CHILDREN:	Children age 7 and older welcome
ANIMALS:	Not allowed
HANDICAPPED:	Handicapped accessible
DIETARY NEEDS:	Will accommodate guests' special dietary needs

Drunken Bananas

Makes 1 Serving

1   banana, unpeeled
Kahlúa, Tia Maria or other coffee-flavored liqueur
Cinnamon-sugar
Ben & Jerry's ice cream

Preheat oven to 350°F. Bake banana in its skin for 15-20 minutes, until black and soft. Cut banana open and serve in its skin with a dash of Kahlúa or Tia Maria and a sprinkle of cinnamon-sugar. Top with ice cream.

Wander Inn

The Wander Inn is located in the quiet Top of the Hill District, within walking distance of Newport's downtown shops and restaurants, Mansion Row and the beach. This small, casually elegant inn combines the grace of Victorian decor with the comfort and convenience of modern amenities. If an upscale setting and fabulous food are important ingredients for your stay, then you will certainly not be disappointed at the Wander Inn.

"The breakfasts are out of this world. Wander Inn is clean, bright and beautiful. We can't wait to come back!" ~ Guests, Wander Inn

INNKEEPERS:	Karen A. Ponce
ADDRESS:	15 Greenough Place
	Newport, Rhode Island 02840
TELEPHONE:	(401) 849-5208; (888) 768-2908
E-MAIL:	karen@wanderinn.com
WEBSITE:	www.wanderinn.com
ROOMS:	2 Rooms; Private baths
CHILDREN:	Children age 12 and older welcome
ANIMALS:	Not allowed; Resident dog
HANDICAPPED:	Not handicapped accessible
DIETARY NEEDS:	Will accommodate guests' special dietary needs

Strawberries Romanoff

Makes 4 to 6 Servings

1	quart strawberries, halved
¼	cup sugar
1	pint strawberry ice cream
½	cup sour cream
2	tablespoons orange liqueur, such as Cointreau or Gran Gala

Sprinkle strawberries with sugar. Cover and chill. Put ice cream in a bowl and stir just to soften. Fold sour cream and orange liqueur into ice cream. Cover and freeze for at least 1 hour or overnight.

When ready to serve, remove ice cream mixture from freezer and let stand at room temperature until somewhat softened. Divide strawberries among bowls and top with a generous dollop of ice cream mixture to serve.

White Rocks Inn

Experience the warmth and charm of old Vermont at the White Rocks Inn Bed & Breakfast, a historic dairy farm. This classic Vermont farmhouse wraps you in warmth from the moment you enter the front door. The view of the mountains and valley from your window is virtually the same as it was in the 1800s.

The inn is central to shopping in the quaint villages along Route 7, scenic trips through the countryside, outdoor activities, downhill skiing at Pico, Okemo or Killington and cross-country skiing on the inn's property.

INNKEEPERS:	Malcolm & Rita Swogger
ADDRESS:	1774 U.S. 7 South
	Wallingford, Vermont 05773
TELEPHONE:	(802) 446-2077; (866) 446-2077
E-MAIL:	info@whiterocksinn.com
WEBSITE:	www.whiterocksinn.com
ROOMS:	5 Rooms; 1 Cottage; Private baths
CHILDREN:	Children welcome; Call ahead
ANIMALS:	Welcome in cottage; Resident dog
HANDICAPPED:	Not handicapped accessible
DIETARY NEEDS:	Will accommodate guests' special dietary needs

Baked Peaches with Raspberries & Cream

Makes 4 Servings

"We serve this a lot in summer when peaches are fresh and plentiful. We nearly always serve it for breakfast the morning after we have a wedding at the inn. It's the perfect tribute to love and happiness. Plan ahead – the peaches need to be refrigerated overnight" - Innkeeper, White Rocks Inn Bed & Breakfast

2	large ripe, firm peaches, peeled, halved and pitted
4	teaspoons raspberry preserves, plus extra for garnish
½	cup heavy cream
2	teaspoons powdered sugar
¼	teaspoon vanilla extract

Whipped cream, for serving
Fresh raspberries, for garnish

Preheat oven to 350°F. Fill each peach cavity with 1 teaspoon of raspberry preserves. Put peaches on a greased baking sheet. Bake for 30-40 minutes, until peaches are very tender, but still hold their shape. Cool, then cover and refrigerate overnight.

The next day, whip together cream, powdered sugar and vanilla just until thick. Spread a pool of cream mixture in each of 4 serving dishes. Place 1 peach half in center of cream in each dish.

With an eyedropper, drop 5 small dots of raspberry jam (thinned with a little water) in cream around edges of dish. Draw the point of a sharp toothpick through each dot of jam, forming tiny hearts (wipe toothpick with a paper towel after forming each heart). Top each peach with a dab of whipped cream and a fresh raspberry.

Honeysuckle Hill

On the edge of the small village of West Barnstable, the circa 1810 Honeysuckle Hill Bed & Breakfast has been welcoming guests for generations. Listed on the National Register of Historic Places, this enchanting seaside inn offers comfortably elegant rooms and graciously served breakfasts. Built in the Queen Anne-style, the inn is surrounded by lush, green lawns and colorful gardens.

Less than two miles from the inn is Sandy Neck, a classic barrier beach that stretches for six miles along Cape Cod Bay.

INNKEEPERS:	Bill & Mary Kilburn
ADDRESS:	591 Main Street, Route 6A
	West Barnstable, Massachusetts 02668
TELEPHONE:	(508) 362-8418
E-MAIL:	stay@honeysucklehill.com
WEBSITE:	www.honeysucklehill.com
ROOMS:	3 Rooms; 1 Suite; Private baths
CHILDREN:	Welcome
ANIMALS:	Not allowed
HANDICAPPED:	Not handicapped accessible
DIETARY NEEDS:	Will accommodate guests' special dietary needs

Bohemian Plum Dumplings

Makes 4 to 6 Servings

"My grandmother was born in Czechoslovakia and came to America in 1923. As a young girl, she studied cooking in Vienna. Although she did not cook 'professionally,' she did prepare wonderful dishes for our family and friends. More importantly, my grandmother grew most of her own food on just two acres of land. My grandfather would go to the store and buy staples, such as coffee beans, flour, salt and sugar, but they grew everything else. They had a summer kitchen and a smoke house on the property. This recipe is from my grandmother. I still have several of her cooking utensils, which I treasure. These dumplings can be served as a side dish for lunch or as a light supper. They can be made with any fruit, such as peaches, but are usually made with fresh or canned plums." ~ Innkeeper, Honeysuckle Hill Bed & Breakfast

1½	pounds potatoes
2	cups all-purpose flour
2	eggs

Salt, to taste
Fresh whole plums or canned plums, drained

Topping:

1	stick butter
½	cup sugar
½	(15-ounce) container dry breadcrumbs (about 2 cups)

Boil potatoes until done, then immediately peel and mash. Add flour, eggs and salt; stir until a dough is formed. Roll out dough on a floured surface. Cut dough into 2-inch squares. Wrap each plum in dough. Drop in boiling water and boil for about 10 minutes. Remove with a slotted spoon and roll in topping. Serve warm.

For the topping: Melt butter in a skillet over medium-low heat. Add sugar and breadcrumbs; mix thoroughly and cook until browned.

Cape Cod Claddagh Inn

Most guests describe their stay at the Cape Cod Claddagh Inn as being like a visit to their grandmother's house. Relax by the fireplace or the pool and enjoy a fabulous homemade meal. Set in the pines, the inn is a quiet and relaxing place for couples.

The inn's Claddagh Pub is a "delightfully Irish," intimate pub serving homemade meals to visitors and Cape Codders alike. Authentic in every detail, the pub has a copper-clad bar, Irish beers and stout, cocktails and pub fare. It is a place where good craic (conversation) prevails.

INNKEEPERS:	Eileen, Jack & Cathy Connell
ADDRESS:	77-79 West Main Street, Route 28
	West Harwich, Massachusetts 02671
TELEPHONE:	(508) 432-9628; (800) 356-9628
E-MAIL:	info@capecodcladdaghinn.com
WEBSITE:	www.capecodcladdaghinn.com
ROOMS:	9 Rooms; Private baths
CHILDREN:	Welcome
ANIMALS:	Call ahead
HANDICAPPED:	Not handicapped accessible
DIETARY NEEDS:	Will accommodate guests' special dietary needs

Claddagh Cranberry Conserve & Chutney

Makes About 3 Cups

"Cape Cod is famous for its cranberries. Our cooks and staff harvest the berries of Harwich each October. It is very hard work. This recipe will make a conserve or a chutney. Use it as a unique accompaniment to most meals." ~ Innkeeper, Cape Cod Claddagh Inn

Conserve:
- 1 (16-ounce) can whole berry cranberry sauce
- ½ cup honey
- ½ cup raisins
- ½ cup chopped walnuts

Chutney:
- 1 teaspoon curry powder, or to taste
- 2 tablespoons balsamic vinegar

For the conserve: Combine all ingredients in a saucepan over medium heat. Bring to a boil, lower heat and simmer for 5 minutes. Serve warm or cold.

For the chutney: Add curry powder and balsamic vinegar to conserve and mix until thoroughly combined.

Marston Family Bed & Breakfast

The Marston Family Bed & Breakfast was built by Winslow Marston in 1786 and is the oldest house in Hyannis Port. The inn is conveniently located near two beautiful, warm saltwater beaches on Nantucket sound. Excellent dining, shopping and entertainment is only a half-mile away. Go on a sightseeing cruise of Hyannis and Hyannis Port Harbors, fish on charter or party boats or catch a ferry to Nantucket or Martha's Vineyard.

Guests are invited to join the innkeepers for a complimentary sailing excursion aboard their 34-foot sailboat, the Catboat Eventide.

INNKEEPERS:	Marcus Sherman & Lynette Furtado
ADDRESS:	70 Marston Avenue
	Hyannis Port, Massachusetts 02647
TELEPHONE:	(508) 775-3334
E-MAIL:	marcus334@hotmail.com
WEBSITE:	www.catboat.com/b&b
ROOMS:	3 Rooms; 1 Suite; Private baths
CHILDREN:	Welcome
ANIMALS:	Dogs & cats welcome; Resident dogs and cat
HANDICAPPED:	Handicapped accessible
DIETARY NEEDS:	Will accommodate guests' special dietary needs

Mango Smoothie

Makes 2 Servings

"This is based on my eight years living in India and Thailand where mangos are common and delicious." ~ Innkeeper, Marston Family Bed & Breakfast

1	ripe mango
3	scoops vanilla ice cream
1	egg (optional)
¾	cup milk
4	ice cubes

Nutmeg, to taste

Blend all ingredients, except nutmeg, in a blender until ice is dissolved. Pour into 2 large glasses. Sprinkle lightly with nutmeg. Serve immediately.

The 1785 Inn

The 1785 Inn is a wonderfully relaxing place to vacation any time of year. The inn's central location puts you in the midst of a wide variety of activities … or just relax at the inn in front of the crackling fire or spend a summer's afternoon by the swimming pool overlooking the mountains. The view from the inn's lawn is one of the most photographed and painted in the country!

The inn features two guest living rooms with original fireplaces, a casual lounge and over six acres of beautiful grounds and gardens to enjoy.

INNKEEPERS:	Becky & Charlie Mallar
ADDRESS:	3582 White Mountain Highway
	North Conway, New Hampshire 03860
TELEPHONE:	(603) 356-9025; (800) 421-1785
E-MAIL:	the1785inn@aol.com
WEBSITE:	www.the1785inn.com
ROOMS:	17 Rooms; 1 Suite; Private & shared baths
CHILDREN:	Welcome
ANIMALS:	Not allowed
HANDICAPPED:	Not handicapped accessible
DIETARY NEEDS:	Will accommodate guests' special dietary needs

Fresh Blueberry Pie

Makes 6 to 8 Servings

Crust (yields 3):
- 4 cups all-purpose flour
- 2 teaspoons salt
- ¾ stick butter, softened
- ½ cup water
- 1 tablespoon vinegar
- 1 large egg

Blueberry sauce:
- 1 cup fresh or frozen blueberries
- 1 cup sugar
- 1 cup water, divided
- ¼ cup all-purpose flour

Filling:
- 1 (8-ounce) package cream cheese, softened
- 3 cups fresh or frozen blueberries
- Sweetened whipped cream, for garnish

For the crust: Preheat oven to 425°F. Butter a pie pan. In a large bowl, combine flour, salt and butter. In a medium bowl, combine water, vinegar and egg. Add egg mixture to flour mixture; combine well. Divide dough into 3 equal parts. Roll out 1 part and place in pie pan (extra dough can be frozen). Bake for 10 minutes, or until done.

For the sauce: Combine blueberries, sugar and ¾ cup of water in a saucepan over medium heat. Bring to a boil, lower heat and simmer until blueberries burst. Combine flour and remaining ¼ cup of water; add to blueberry mixture. Cook, stirring, for 2-3 minutes, until sauce thickens.

For the filling and to serve: Spread a thin layer of cream cheese over bottom of crust. Sprinkle 1½ cups of blueberries over cream cheese. Top with ⅓-½ of blueberry sauce. Top with remaining 1½ cups of blueberries. Top with remaining sauce. Chill for at least 1 hour. Serve topped with a dollop of sweetened whipped cream flavored with a little vanilla.

The Combes Family Inn

The Combes Family Inn Bed & Breakfast is a true family inn situated on a quiet country back road in the heart of Vermont's mountain and lake region. You are invited to explore the inn's 50 acres of rolling meadows and woods and to take advantage of the skiing, foliage, hiking and much more. Enjoy hearty, home-cooked meals, spectacular views, a roaring fire on a cold night or a stroll along country back roads on a summer evening.

When the dinner bell rings, a three-course, home-cooked meal is served that is "like going to your Grandmother's house for Sunday dinner."

INNKEEPERS:	Ruth & Bill Combes
ADDRESS:	953 East Lake Road
	Ludlow, Vermont 05149
TELEPHONE:	(802) 228-8799; (800) 822-8799
E-MAIL:	info@combesfamilyinn.com
WEBSITE:	www.combesfamilyinn.com
ROOMS:	11 Rooms; Private baths
CHILDREN:	Welcome
ANIMALS:	Welcome; Resident dog
HANDICAPPED:	Not handicapped accessible
DIETARY NEEDS:	Will accommodate guests' special dietary needs

Sour Cream Rhubarb Streusel Pie

Makes 8 Servings

"Our inn has a very large rhubarb patch. I make and freeze endless strawberry rhubarb pies, but the following sour cream rhubarb pie is also a very popular dessert at the inn." ~ Innkeeper, The Combes Family Inn

1	cup sour cream
1	large egg
¾	cup sugar
2	tablespoons all-purpose flour
¼	teaspoon salt
1	teaspoon vanilla extract
3	cups chopped rhubarb

Ice cream, for serving

Streusel topping:

½	cup packed brown sugar
⅓	cup old-fashioned rolled oats
½	stick butter, softened
1	teaspoon cinnamon

Preheat oven to 350°F. Beat together sour cream and egg. Add sugar, flour, salt and vanilla. Stir in rhubarb. Pour into an 8x8-inch baking pan. Sprinkle with topping. Bake for 30-35 minutes. Serve with ice cream.

For the topping: Combine all topping ingredients.

Beal House Inn

Located in New Hampshire's majestic White Mountains, the Beal House Inn is an ideal home base for day trips to explore the surrounding area and major attractions. North of the Notch, the inn is free from the congestion and commercialism of city life and ski lodge sprawl.

Delicious breakfasts and desserts are made in-house. The inn's fine dining restaurant features a mix of classic cuisine and one of the most impressive martini menus around. Chef Jose Luis was recognized as one of the "Top 15 Chefs in an Inn" in 2004 by Arrington's Bed & Breakfast Journal.

INNKEEPERS:	Catherine & Jose Luis Pawelek
ADDRESS:	2 West Main Street
	Littleton, New Hampshire 03561
TELEPHONE:	(603) 444-2661; (888) 616-2325
E-MAIL:	info@bealhouseinn.com
WEBSITE:	www.bealhouseinn.com
ROOMS:	3 Rooms; 5 Suites; Private baths
CHILDREN:	Children age 8 and older welcome
ANIMALS:	Small dogs allowed; Resident dogs
HANDICAPPED:	Handicapped accessible; Call ahead
DIETARY NEEDS:	Will accommodate guests' special dietary needs

Catherine's Tarte Tatin

Makes 8 Servings

"Besides apple and peach, try the following combinations: pear and nectarine; apple and banana; pear and mango; apple and plum; or pear and kiwi." - Innkeeper, Beal House Inn & Restaurant

3	peaches, peeled and quartered
6	large apples (Red Delicious or Granny Smith), peeled and quartered
3	tablespoons all-purpose flour
½	cup sugar
1	teaspoon butter
1	teaspoon vanilla extract
1	(8-ounce) package puff pastry

Sorbet or ice cream, for serving

Preheat oven to 350°F. Trim puff pastry sheet into a circle; roll it out on a lightly floured surface into a 12-inch round. Let puff pastry come to room temperature.

Combine sugar and vanilla in a 10-inch, oven-proof skillet over medium heat. Cook, stirring occasionally, for about 4-5 minutes, until mixture turns a caramel color (be careful not to overcook, or sugar will burn). Remove pan from heat.

Place 1 layer of fruit on its side, back to front, alternating peaches and ½ of apples, atop caramel in skillet (be careful – pan and caramel will be very hot). Make a second layer using remaining apples (this will give the tart some height to support the puff pastry). Drape puff pastry sheet over top of skillet, crimping edges into pan rim.

Transfer skillet to oven and bake for 30-40 minutes, until top of pastry is golden brown and crisp. Remove from oven and let stand for 4-5 minutes, then invert tart onto a large plate. Serve warm with sorbet or ice cream.

Brewster By The Sea

As you approach Brewster By The Sea Bed & Breakfast, a sense of graciousness and gentility abounds. This award-winning, romantic country inn is one of Cape Cod's finest bed & breakfasts. Situated in the heart of Brewster's historic district, the inn's convenient Main Street location belies the peaceful solitude of this expansive property, replete with outdoor pool, whirlpool spa, gardens and orchard.

Breakfast is a feast for the eye and the palate, made fresh each day from the finest ingredients, including herbs from the inn's garden.

INNKEEPERS:	Donna & Byron Cain
ADDRESS:	716 Main Street
	Brewster, Massachusetts 02631
TELEPHONE:	(508) 896-3910; (800) 892-3910
E-MAIL:	stay@brewsterbythesea.com
WEBSITE:	www.brewsterbythesea.com
ROOMS:	7 Rooms; 2 Suites; Private baths
CHILDREN:	Children age 12 and older welcome
ANIMALS:	Not allowed; Resident dog
HANDICAPPED:	Not handicapped accessible
DIETARY NEEDS:	Will accommodate guests' special dietary needs

Plum Torte

Makes 8 Servings

"Italian plums make this a delicious fall treat. Peaches or apples may be substituted for the plums. ~ Innkeeper, Brewster by the Sea

1	stick unsalted butter
1	cup sugar, plus extra for topping
1	cup all-purpose flour, sifted
1	teaspoon baking powder

Pinch of salt

2	eggs
12	Italian plums, halved and pitted

Lemon juice, to taste

1   teaspoon cinnamon

Whipped cream and/or ice cream, for serving

Preheat oven to 350°F. Cream together butter and sugar. Add flour, baking powder, salt and eggs; beat well. Spoon butter mixture into a greased 9-inch springform pan. Place plums, skin-side-up, on top of batter. Sprinkle plums lightly with sugar and lemon juice. Sprinkle with cinnamon. Bake torte for 1 hour. Serve with whipped cream and/or ice cream.

The Sherburne Inn

The Sherburne Inn Bed & Breakfast is tucked away in a quiet corner of beautiful Nantucket. Built in 1835 as the headquarters for the Atlantic Silk Company, the inn is ideally located just minutes from Main Street and a short five minute walk from Steamboat Wharf. The inn's rich history and original artworks enhance the warmth and beauty felt by guests.

Each morning, a delicious home-baked continental plus breakfast is served, complete with homemade muffins and Nantucket-made breads.

INNKEEPERS:	Susan & Dale Hamilton
ADDRESS:	10 Gay Street
	Nantucket, Massachusetts 02554
TELEPHONE:	(508) 228-4425; (888) 577-4425
E-MAIL:	sherinn@nantucket.net
WEBSITE:	www.sherburneinn.com
ROOMS:	8 Rooms; Private baths
CHILDREN:	Children age 6 and older welcome
ANIMALS:	Not allowed
HANDICAPPED:	Not handicapped accessible
DIETARY NEEDS:	Will accommodate guests' special dietary needs

Nantucket Cranberry Apple Crisp

Makes 18 Servings

6	cups chopped peeled tart apple
4	cups cranberries, fresh or frozen
2	cups white sugar
3	cups old-fashioned rolled oats
2	sticks butter, melted
1	cup light brown sugar
⅔	cup all-purpose flour

Ice cream, for serving (optional)

Preheat oven to 350°F. Combine apples, cranberries and white sugar in a saucepan over medium heat; cook until cranberries pop or until apples have softened slightly and there is still liquid in pan. Spread apple mixture in a lightly buttered 9x13-inch baking dish.

Combine oats, butter, brown sugar and flour; sprinkle over apple mixture. Bake for 30 minutes, or until top is lightly browned and apple mixture is bubbling. Serve warm with ice cream, if desired.

Desserts

Double Chocolate Chip Cookies 265

Coconut Chocolate Chip Cookies 267

Crunchy Chocolate Chip Cookies 269

Maple Butter Cookies 271

Gingerbread Mascarpone Petite Fours...273

Chocolate Raspberry Almond Delights.......................................275

Chocolate Walnut Espresso Biscotti 277

Chocolate Walnut Bars 279

"Oh Henry" Bars 281

1811 House Brownies...283

Primrose Coconut "Joys" 285

Malbone Butter Cake 287

Rum Cake 289

Egg Nog Cheesecake Cake 291

Pumpkin Layer Cheesecake 293

Pumpkin Whoopie Pies 295

Maine Maple Syrup Pie 297

Larchwood Pie 299

Coconut Mousse with Clara Gold's Butterscotch Sauce 301

Chocolate Chambord Soufflé 303

Desserts

Inn at Crystal Lake

The Inn at Crystal Lake's Palmer House Pub has been recognized by *The Boston Globe* as the perfect spot to relax with a drink and some delicious food after a day exploring the area's stunning landscapes. Take a seat at the gorgeous walnut bar, originally from Boston's Ritz-Carlton, or snuggle up by woodstove. In summer, sit on the patio with a glass of wine.

Each season offers unique ways to experience the White Mountains and Lakes Region, and the Inn at Crystal Lake keeps you close to everything. From water sports to fall foliage tours, the Inn at Crystal Lake has it all!

INNKEEPERS:	Bobby Barker & Tim Ostendorf
ADDRESS:	Route 153
	Eaton Center, New Hampshire 03832
TELEPHONE:	(603) 447-2120; (800) 343-7336
E-MAIL:	stay@innatcrystallake.com
WEBSITE:	www.innatcrystallake.com
ROOMS:	11 Rooms; 1 Cottage; Private baths
CHILDREN:	Children age 10 and older welcome
ANIMALS:	Dogs welcome (1 room); Resident cats
HANDICAPPED:	Not handicapped accessible
DIETARY NEEDS:	Will accommodate guests' special dietary needs

Double Chocolate Chip Cookies

Makes 50 to 55 Cookies

"Add raisins or dried cranberries for a truly 'loaded' cookie." ~ Innkeeper, Inn at Crystal Lake

2½	cups old-fashioned rolled oats
2	sticks butter, softened
1	cup white sugar
1	cup packed brown sugar
2	eggs
1	teaspoon vanilla extract
2	cups all-purpose flour
½	teaspoon salt
1	teaspoon baking powder
1	teaspoon baking soda
1	(4-ounce) Hershey bar, melted
12	ounces semi-sweet chocolate chips
1½	cups chopped walnuts
1½	cups raisins or dried cranberries (optional)

Preheat oven to 350°F. Blend oatmeal in a blender or food processor to a fine powder. In a large bowl, cream together butter, white sugar and brown sugar. Mix in eggs and vanilla. In a medium bowl, combine oats, flour, salt, baking powder and baking soda; add to butter mixture and mix well. Add melted Hershey bar and mix until well combined. Stir in chocolate chips, nuts and raisins or dried cranberries, if desired. Roll dough into balls and place 2-inches apart on a cookie sheet. Bake for 10 minutes.

Brewster By The Sea

Brewster by the Sea is a quaint bed & breakfast located in the historic sea captains' town of Brewster on Cape Cod. Five beautiful, Old World rooms are located in the Olde Farmhouse, which was built around 1846. Brewster is centrally located on Cape Cod, where you will find numerous antique stores, art galleries, museums and specialty boutiques to explore.

Breakfast is a special time at the inn. Begin the morning sipping coffee to classical music in the gathering room, then enjoy a leisurely breakfast on the veranda overlooking the tropical pool with waterfall.

INNKEEPERS:	Donna & Byron Cain
ADDRESS:	716 Main Street
	Brewster, Massachusetts 02631
TELEPHONE:	(508) 896-3910; (800) 892-3910
E-MAIL:	stay@brewsterbythesea.com
WEBSITE:	www.brewsterbythesea.com
ROOMS:	7 Rooms; 2 Suites; Private baths
CHILDREN:	Children age 12 and older welcome
ANIMALS:	Not allowed; Resident dog
HANDICAPPED:	Not handicapped accessible
DIETARY NEEDS:	Will accommodate guests' special dietary needs

Coconut Chocolate Chip Cookies

Makes 36 Cookies

"A new rendition of the traditional chocolate chip cookie. These never last long in the cookie jar!" ~ Innkeeper, Brewster by the Sea

1½	cups crushed graham crackers
½	cup all-purpose flour
2	teaspoons baking powder
1	stick butter, softened
1	(14-ounce) can sweetened condensed milk
1⅓	cups shredded coconut
1½	cups chocolate chips
1	cup chopped walnuts

Preheat oven to 375°F. In a medium bowl, combine graham crackers, flour and baking powder. In a large bowl, beat butter and sweetened condensed milk with a mixer until smooth; add to flour mixture and mix well. Stir in coconut, chocolate chips and walnuts. Drop dough by rounded teaspoonful onto a lightly greased cookie sheet. Bake cookies for 9-10 minutes, until lightly browned.

1811 House

Exquisitely maintained, this former home of Abraham Lincoln's granddaughter features the warmth and detail of Federal-period styling. Fireplaces, canopied beds, private porches, fine Oriental rugs, authentic antiques and prized artworks are among the features that make the 1811 House perfect for those seeking casual sophistication. Each guest room features fluffy robes, comfortable chairs and fine bath amenities.

An authentic British pub, featuring over 70 single malt scotches, greets guests seeking a "toddy" by the fireplace or at the rich wood bar.

INNKEEPERS:	Marnie & Bruce Duff and Cathy & Jorge Veleta
ADDRESS:	3654 Main Street
	Manchester, Vermont 05254
TELEPHONE:	(802) 362-1811; (800) 432-1811
E-MAIL:	info@1811house.com
WEBSITE:	www.1811house.com
ROOMS:	11 Rooms; 2 Suites; Private baths
CHILDREN:	Children age 16 and older welcome
ANIMALS:	Not allowed
HANDICAPPED:	Not handicapped accessible
DIETARY NEEDS:	Will accommodate guests' special dietary needs

Crunchy Chocolate Chip Cookies

Makes 40 Cookies

1	stick butter, softened
1	stick margarine, softened
1	cup packed brown sugar
1	cup white sugar
1	large egg
2	teaspoons vanilla extract
3½	cups all-purpose flour
1	tablespoon baking soda
1	teaspoon salt
1	cup vegetable oil
1½	cups corn flakes
1½	cups quick-cooking oats
1	(12-ounce) package chocolate chips

Preheat oven to 350°F. In a large bowl, cream together butter, margarine and brown and white sugar. Beat in egg and vanilla. In a medium bowl, combine flour, baking soda and salt. Alternately stir flour mixture and vegetable oil into butter mixture until thoroughly combined. Stir in corn flakes, oats and chocolate chips. Chill dough for about 1 hour.

Drop dough by heaping tablespoonsful (or use a small ice cream scoop), 3-inches apart, onto an ungreased cookie sheet (drop dough by teaspoonsful for smaller cookies). Bake for 13-14 minutes, until golden brown. Cool on wire racks.

The Birds Nest Inn

Called "Vermont's best-kept secret," the Birds Nest Inn is Waterbury's only AAA Three Diamond, Mobil Three Star bed & breakfast. In addition to superb gourmet breakfasts and access to a plethora of summer and winter activities, the inn's "wine corner" offers guests an introduction to distinct and rare wines from around the world.

Waterbury offers visitors an array of year-round activities, from antiquing, shopping and outdoor sports to music festivals, theatre productions, car shows and an Oktoberfest celebration.

INNKEEPERS:	Len, Nancy & Valerie Vignola
ADDRESS:	5088 Waterbury-Stowe Road
	Waterbury Center, Vermont 05677
TELEPHONE:	(802) 244-7490; (800) 366-5592
E-MAIL:	nestlein@birdsnestinn.com
WEBSITE:	www.birdsnestinn.com
ROOMS:	6 Rooms; Private baths
CHILDREN:	Not allowed
ANIMALS:	Not allowed; Resident dogs
HANDICAPPED:	Not handicapped accessible
DIETARY NEEDS:	Will accommodate guests' special dietary needs

Maple Butter Cookies

Makes About 24 Cookies

1½	sticks butter, softened
½	cup firmly packed brown sugar
1	large egg
½	cup Vermont maple syrup
1	teaspoon maple flavoring or maple extract (optional)
2¼	cups all-purpose flour
2	teaspoons baking powder
½	teaspoon baking soda
24	walnut halves (about)

Preheat oven to 400°F. Cream butter thoroughly. Gradually add brown sugar and beat until fluffy. Add egg, maple syrup, maple flavoring, flour, baking powder and baking soda; beat well. Drop dough by rounded teaspoonful on an ungreased cookie sheet. Top each cookie with a walnut half. Bake cookies for 8-10 minutes.

Gateways Inn

The Gateways Inn will transport you to another time and place. The incomparable elegance of the Procter mansion, infused with European charm and hospitality, is truly enchanting. Located in the heart of Lenox, in the Berkshire Hills, the inn offers a perfect getaway for any occasion.

The restaurant at the Gateways Inn, among the finest in Lenox, exudes luxury and comfort amid linen-covered tables, silver candlesticks and fresh flowers. Glass doors open into the main dining room, with its deep terra cotta painted walls hung with antique Italian and European prints.

INNKEEPERS:	Fabrizio & Rosemary Chiariello
ADDRESS:	51 Walker Street
	Lenox, Massachusetts 01240
TELEPHONE:	(413) 637-2532; (888) 492-9466
E-MAIL:	gateways@berkshire.net
WEBSITE:	www.gatewaysinn.com
ROOMS:	11 Rooms; 1 Suite; Private baths
CHILDREN:	Children age 10 and older welcome
ANIMALS:	Not allowed
HANDICAPPED:	Not handicapped accessible
DIETARY NEEDS:	Will accommodate guests' special dietary needs

Gingerbread Mascarpone Petite Fours

Makes About 24 Petite Fours

6	large eggs
1	pound brown sugar
2½	cups all-purpose flour
2	tablespoons baking powder
1	teaspoon baking soda
1	teaspoon salt
4	tablespoons cinnamon
3	tablespoons molasses
3	sticks butter, melted
½	cup half & half
¾	cup buttermilk
½	pound white chocolate, shaved, plus ½ pound white chocolate, melted
2	pounds mascarpone cheese
2	tablespoons powdered sugar

Preheat oven to 350°F. In a large bowl, beat eggs and sugar until foamy. Sift together flour, baking powder, baking soda, salt and cinnamon into a small bowl; stir into egg mixture. In a bowl, mix molasses, butter, half & half and buttermilk; stir into egg mixture. Spread batter in a greased and floured jelly roll pan. Bake for about 15 minutes, or until gingerbread is springy and a toothpick inserted in center comes out clean. With a long, serrated knife, slice gingerbread in half horizontally. Carefully separate layers.

Mix shaved white chocolate and mascarpone cheese with a stand mixer using the paddle attachment for about 5 minutes, until light and fluffy. Mix in powdered sugar. Spread mascarpone mixture over bottom layer of gingerbread. Top with top layer of gingerbread. Cut into 1-inch squares or diamonds. Put petite fours on a wire rack placed on a baking sheet. Coat petite fours with melted white chocolate. Let chocolate set, then repeat to thoroughly and evenly coat.

The Winslow House

The Winslow House is a beautifully restored, circa 1790 farmhouse. The inn is decorated with a 25-year collection of early American antiques, charming New England accent pieces and a unique contemporary flair. Located a mile from the Village "Green," the inn is just minutes from Woodstock's many attractions, galleries, restaurants and outdoor activities.

The inn's creative breakfasts blend international style with traditional New England country cuisine. Dishes include Mt. Tom peach waffles and the Green Mountain frittata with Vermont cheddar cheese and smoked ham.

INNKEEPERS:	Tod & Jen Minotti
ADDRESS:	492 Woodstock Road
	Woodstock, Vermont 05091
TELEPHONE:	(802) 457-1820 ; (866) 457-1820
E-MAIL:	info@thewinslowhousevt.com
WEBSITE:	www.thewinslowhousevt.com
ROOMS:	1 Rooms; 3 Suites; Private baths
CHILDREN:	Children age 8 and older welcome
ANIMALS:	Welcome; On-site boarding
HANDICAPPED:	Not handicapped accessible
DIETARY NEEDS:	Will accommodate guests' special dietary needs

Chocolate Raspberry Almond Delights

Makes 20 to 24 Cookies

2	sticks butter or margarine, softened
1	cup brown sugar
½	cup white sugar
2	large eggs
1½	teaspoons almond extract
1	small drop orange extract
2	teaspoons baking powder
½	teaspoon salt
2	cups all-purpose flour
2	cups old-fashioned or quick-cooking rolled oats
¾	cup raspberry chips or fresh raspberries
¾	cup chocolate chips
1	cup sliced or chopped almonds

Preheat oven to 350°F. In a large bowl, mix butter and brown sugar and white sugar until creamy. Mix in eggs. Mix in almond and orange extract, baking powder and salt. Stir in flour and oats. Mix in raspberry and chocolate chips and almonds.

Roll dough into balls and place on an ungreased cookie sheet. Bake for 12 minutes, or until golden on bottom (do not over bake – cookies should appear gooey and slightly underbaked). Cool slightly on cookie sheet, then transfer to a wire rack.

Harborside House

The Harborside House offers gracious accommodations and warm hospitality in an ideal location. This handsome, circa 1850 home in Marblehead's historic district overlooks picturesque Marblehead Harbor. Guests enjoy water views from the wood-paneled parlor, dining room and summer breakfast porch. Guest rooms feature antique furnishings and period wallpaper.

Only a short walk from the inn are antique shops, art galleries and shops of local craftsmen, as well as a dining choices to suit every taste and budget.

INNKEEPERS:	Susan Livingston
ADDRESS:	23 Gregory Street
	Marblehead, Massachusetts 01945
TELEPHONE:	(781) 631-1032
E-MAIL:	stay@harborsidehouse.com
WEBSITE:	www.harborsidehouse.com
ROOMS:	2 Rooms; Shared baths
CHILDREN:	Children age 8 and older welcome
ANIMALS:	Not allowed
HANDICAPPED:	Not handicapped accessible
DIETARY NEEDS:	Will accommodate guests' special dietary needs

Chocolate Walnut Espresso Biscotti

Makes 30 Biscotti

2	cups unbleached all-purpose flour
1	cup sugar
½	teaspoon baking powder
½	teaspoon baking soda
½	teaspoon salt
½	teaspoon cinnamon
¼	teaspoon ground cloves
¼	cup plus 1 tablespoon strong brewed coffee, cooled
1	tablespoon plus 1 teaspoon milk
1	large egg
1	teaspoon vanilla extract
1¼	cups chocolate chips
¾	cup chopped walnuts (or almonds or pistachios)
¾	cup dried cranberries

Preheat oven to 350°F. In a large bowl, combine flour, sugar, baking powder, baking soda, salt, cinnamon and cloves. In a small bowl, combine coffee, milk, egg and vanilla; add to flour mixture and mix until flour is moistened (add a few more drops of coffee, if needed). Stir in chocolate chips, walnuts and dried cranberries.

On a well-floured surface, form dough into 3½-inch-long, ½-inch-thick flat logs. Transfer logs to a greased and floured cookie sheet. Bake for about 20 minutes. Remove from oven and cool. Cut logs into ½-inch-thick slices. Lay slices cut-side-down on cookie sheet. Lower oven temperature to 300°F. Bake for 6-8 minutes (for crisper biscotti, turn and bake for 6-8 minutes longer).

The Francis Malbone House

The Francis Malbone House estate was built in 1760 for Colonel Francis Malbone, who made his fortune as a shipping merchant. The mansion has been lovingly maintained and restored through the years. Each luxurious guestroom is tastefully decorated with Colonial antiques and period reproductions. With its downtown harborfront location, the inn is within walking distance of nearly all of Newport's attractions.

Newport's only Five Star Diamond Award-winning inn, the inn was rated "Extraordinary" in *Zagat's 2002 Top U.S. Hotels, Resorts and Spas.*

INNKEEPERS:	Will Dewey and Mark & Jasminka Eads
ADDRESS:	392 Thames Street
	Newport, Rhode Island 02840
TELEPHONE:	(401) 846-0392; (800) 846-0392
E-MAIL:	innkeeper@malbone.com
WEBSITE:	www.malbone.com
ROOMS:	17 Rooms; 3 Suites; Private baths
CHILDREN:	Children age 12 and older welcome
ANIMALS:	Not allowed
HANDICAPPED:	Handicapped accessible
DIETARY NEEDS:	Will accommodate guests' special dietary needs

Chocolate Walnut Bars

Makes 24 Bars

Crust:
- 1½ cups all-purpose flour
- 1 stick butter or margarine, softened
- ¼ cup packed brown sugar

Filling:
- 3 large eggs
- ¾ cup light corn syrup
- ¾ cup sugar
- 2 tablespoons butter or margarine, melted
- 1 teaspoon vanilla extract
- 1 (12-ounce) package semi-sweet chocolate chips
- 1½ cups coarsely chopped walnuts

For the crust: Preheat oven to 350°F. Beat together flour, butter and brown sugar until crumbly; press into bottom of a greased 9x13-inch baking pan. Bake for 12-15 minutes, or until lightly browned.

For the filling: Beat together eggs, corn syrup, sugar, butter and vanilla. Stir in chocolate chips and walnuts. Pour filling over hot crust. Bake for 25-30 minutes, or until center is set. Cool completely in pan on a wire rack, then cut into bars.

Yankee Clipper Inn

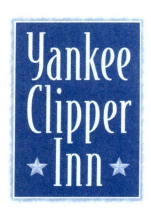

The seaside village of Rockport, with its views of Gloucester, attracts visitors from around the world. The Yankee Clipper Inn, overlooking the ocean, provides the perfect backdrop for a New England getaway. Jackie and John F. Kennedy, John Lennon and Yoko Ono and numerous other celebrities have all been guests of the inn.

Rolling lawns and country gardens frame colorful vistas to the open sea. Breathe deeply the salt air from the gazebo. Relax under the umbrellas on the terrace or swim laps in the sun-filled, heated, salt water pool.

INNKEEPERS:	Randy & Cathy Marks
ADDRESS:	127 Granite Street
	Rockport, Massachusetts 01966
TELEPHONE:	(978) 546-3407; (800) 545-3699
E-MAIL:	info@yankeeclipperinn.com
WEBSITE:	www.yankeeclipperinn.com
ROOMS:	13 Rooms; 3 Suites; Private baths
CHILDREN:	Welcome
ANIMALS:	Not allowed; Resident dogs
HANDICAPPED:	Not handicapped accessible
DIETARY NEEDS:	Will accommodate guests' special dietary needs

"Oh Henry" Bars

Makes 36 Bars

"This is a family recipe. They are messy and delicious. Refrigerate them if you like." ~ Innkeeper, Yankee Clipper Inn

1	stick plus 2⅔ tablespoons butter, softened
1	cup packed brown sugar
½	cup white Karo syrup
1	tablespoon vanilla extract
4	cups old-fashioned rolled oats
¾	cup peanut butter
1	(6-ounce) package chocolate chips

Preheat oven to 350°F. Cream together butter and sugar. Add Karo syrup, vanilla and oats. Spread into a greased 9x13-inch baking pan. Bake for 18-20 minutes.

Melt peanut butter and chocolate chips over low heat on top of double boiler. Spread peanut butter mixture on top of baked layer in pan. Cut into bars while still slightly warm.

1811 House

The 1811 House is centrally located with easy access to Manchester's renowned shopping, golf, restaurants, southern Vermont ski areas including Bromley and Stratton Mountain, and cross-country ski centers such as Hildene and Wild Wings. Yet the views overlooking the Equinox Golf Course encourage guests to spend the day relaxing at the inn. This is truly an East Coast getaway worth enjoying.

Each morning, guests are seated on Chippendale chairs for a gourmet breakfast served on fine china with sterling silver utensils.

INNKEEPERS:	Marnie & Bruce Duff and Cathy & Jorge Veleta
ADDRESS:	3654 Main Street
	Manchester, Vermont 05254
TELEPHONE:	(802) 362-1811; (800) 432-1811
E-MAIL:	info@1811house.com
WEBSITE:	www.1811house.com
ROOMS:	11 Rooms; 2 Suites; Private baths
CHILDREN:	Children age 16 and older welcome
ANIMALS:	Not allowed
HANDICAPPED:	Not handicapped accessible
DIETARY NEEDS:	Will accommodate guests' special dietary needs

1811 House Brownies

Makes About 24 Brownies

4	(1-ounce) squares unsweetened chocolate
2	sticks butter
2	cups sugar
4	large eggs
1	tablespoon brewed strong coffee (optional)
1	cup all-purpose flour
1	teaspoon baking powder
1	(6-ounce) package chocolate chips
1	cup chopped walnuts

Preheat oven to 350°F. Melt chocolate and butter together in a saucepan over medium-low heat. In a large bowl, beat sugar and eggs until ribbons form. Stir in chocolate mixture. Add coffee, if desired. In a small bowl, combine flour and baking powder; stir into batter. Spread batter into a greased 9x13-inch baking pan. Sprinkle with chocolate chips and nuts. Bake for 30 minutes.

Primrose Inn

The Primrose Inn, located on the Historic Corridor in downtown Bar Harbor, is just a short stroll to the Village Green and the Town Pier. When not enjoying the relaxing atmosphere of the inn or shopping in town, guests find outdoor adventure less than a mile away in magnificent Acadia National Park, with its renowned hiking trails and breathtaking, unparalleled scenery.

The inn's delightful afternoon tea features fresh, home-baked treats. It is so popular, many guests plan their day around returning to the inn for tea time!

INNKEEPERS:	Pamela Parker & Bryan Stevens
ADDRESS:	73 Mount Desert Street
	Bar Harbor, Maine 04609
TELEPHONE:	(207) 288-4031; (877) 846-3424
E-MAIL:	relax@primroseinn.com
WEBSITE:	www.primroseinn.com
ROOMS:	11 Rooms; 4 Suites; Private baths
CHILDREN:	Children welcome in suites
ANIMALS:	Not allowed; Resident dog
HANDICAPPED:	Not handicapped accessible
DIETARY NEEDS:	Cannot accommodate guests' special dietary needs

Primrose Coconut "Joys"

Makes About 36

"For a less sweet candy, use half unsweetened coconut. Also, use half semi-sweet chocolate chips for a richer flavor." ~ Innkeeper, Primrose Inn

1	(14-ounce) package sweetened coconut
2/3	cup sugar
6	tablespoons all-purpose flour
1/4	teaspoon salt
4	egg whites
1	teaspoon almond extract (optional)
36	whole almonds, about
1 1/3	cups milk chocolate chips

Preheat oven to 325°F. Combine coconut, sugar, flour and salt. Stir in egg whites and almond extract. Cover and chill for 20-30 minutes.

Encase each almond in enough coconut mixture to form 1-inch balls. Rinse hands in cold water, if necessary, to keep coconut mixture from sticking to fingers. Put coconut balls on a parchment paper-lined baking sheet. Bake for about 20 minutes, until lightly browned. Cool completely on a wire rack.

Melt chocolate chips for 1-2 minutes in a microwave and stir until smooth. Dip tops of coconut balls in melted chocolate. Chill for about 20 minutes, until chocolate is set. Store in an air-tight container with waxed paper between layers.

The Francis Malbone House

Come experience the Francis Malbone House, Newport's most luxurious bed & breakfast. This historic inn, an elegantly restored, circa 1760 Colonial Newport mansion, offers beautiful bedrooms, gracious sitting rooms and manicured gardens. Located in the heart of Newport's historic harborfront, the Francis Malbone House is the epitome of elegance. The innkeepers' personal attention to guests and their needs is unparalleled.

"In a city where bed & breakfasts set national standards, the Francis Malbone House is outstanding." ~ *Gourmet* magazine

INNKEEPERS:	Will Dewey and Mark & Jasminka Eads
ADDRESS:	392 Thames Street
	Newport, Rhode Island 02840
TELEPHONE:	(401) 846-0392; (800) 846-0392
E-MAIL:	innkeeper@malbone.com
WEBSITE:	www.malbone.com
ROOMS:	17 Rooms; 3 Suites; Private baths
CHILDREN:	Children age 12 and older welcome
ANIMALS:	Not allowed
HANDICAPPED:	Handicapped accessible
DIETARY NEEDS:	Will accommodate guests' special dietary needs

Malbone Butter Cake

Makes 1 Bundt Cake

Cake:
- 2   cups sugar
- 2   sticks butter, softened
- 2   teaspoons rum extract or rum
- 4   large eggs
- 3   cups all-purpose flour
- 1   teaspoon baking powder
- ½   teaspoon baking soda
- 1   cup buttermilk or sour milk*

Powdered sugar, for garnish

Rum sauce:
- ¾   cup sugar
- 5⅓   tablespoons butter
- 3   tablespoons water
- 1-2   teaspoons rum extract or 2 tablespoons dark rum

For the cake: Preheat oven to 325°F. Generously grease and lightly flour a 12-cup Bundt pan. Cream together sugar and butter. Add rum extract and eggs; mix well. Add remaining ingredients, except powdered sugar. Beat with a mixer on low speed until moistened, then beat on medium speed for 3 minutes. Pour batter into pan. Bake for 55-70 minutes, or until a toothpick inserted in center comes out clean.

With a long-tined fork or a long toothpick, pierce cake 10-12 times. Slowly pour hot rum sauce over warm cake. Let stand for 5-10 minutes, or until sauce is absorbed. Invert cake onto a serving plate. Cool for 90 minutes, or until a toothpick inserted in center comes out clean. Just before serving, sprinkle with powdered sugar.

For the sauce: Combine sauce ingredients in a saucepan over low heat. Cook, stirring occasionally, until butter in melted and combined (do not boil).

Note: To make 1 cup of sour milk, stir 1½ tablespoons of white vinegar into 1 cup of milk. Let stand in a warm place for 20 minutes.

Golden Slipper

The Golden Slipper – Boston's Bed & Breakfast 'Afloat' – is a 1960 Chris Craft cabin cruiser docked at Lewis Wharf in the heart of Boston's historic North End. Quincy Market, Faneuil Hall Marketplace, the New England Aquarium, historic monuments and museums, the trolley and Boston's Little Italy are all within a ten minute walk.

This romantic accommodation offers excellent views of busy Boston Harbor and the ocean beyond. The Golden Slipper can accommodate up to four guests, with a continental breakfast left for you on the deck of the boat.

INNKEEPERS:	Gretchen & Jack Stephenson
ADDRESS:	Lewis Wharf
	Boston, Massachusetts 02190
TELEPHONE:	(781) 545-2845
E-MAIL:	None available
WEBSITE:	www.bostonsbedandbreakfastafloat.com
ROOMS:	40' Chris Craft (sleeps up to 4); Shared bath
CHILDREN:	Welcome
ANIMALS:	Not allowed
HANDICAPPED:	Not handicapped accessible
DIETARY NEEDS:	Will accommodate guests' special dietary needs

Rum Cake

Makes 10 Servings

"This is a favorite dessert of our charter guests." ~ Innkeeper, The Golden Slipper – Boston's Bed & Breakfast Afloat

1	(18¼-ounce) package yellow cake mix
1	(4½-ounce) package instant vanilla pudding
½	cup water
½	cup vegetable oil
½	cup rum
4	large eggs

Rum sauce:

1	stick butter
½	cup sugar
¾	cup rum
¼	cup water

Preheat oven to 350°F. Combine cake mix, pudding mix, water, oil and rum. Beat in eggs, 1 at a time. Pour batter into a greased Bundt pan. Bake for 1 hour, or until a toothpick inserted in center comes out clean. Remove cake from oven and poke holes in it with a toothpick. Pour rum sauce slowly over cake. Cool cake for about 30 minutes, then slice and serve.

For the rum sauce: Just before cake is done baking, combine butter, sugar, rum and water in a small saucepan over low heat. Cook, stirring, until butter is melted and combined and sugar is dissolved.

Austin Hill Inn

Located in the foothills of the Green Mountains, two miles from Mount Snow Ski Resort and just outside the historic village of West Dover, the Austin Hill Inn offers romantic guestrooms with country appointments, fireplaces and balconies.

Come for the hearty country breakfasts by the fire, the ski packages and the spa vacations. In summer, enjoy the local Marlboro Music Festival or the hilarity of the Murder Mystery Weekends. In fall, relish the natural beauty of Vermont's world-renowned foliage.

INNKEEPERS:	Debbie & John Bailey
ADDRESS:	Route 100
	West Dover, Vermont 05356
TELEPHONE:	(800) 332-7352
E-MAIL:	info@austinhillinn.com
WEBSITE:	www.austinhillinn.com
ROOMS:	10 Rooms; 1 Suite; Private baths
CHILDREN:	Children age 5 and older welcome
ANIMALS:	Dogs allowed (up to 50 pounds); Resident dogs
HANDICAPPED:	Not handicapped accessible
DIETARY NEEDS:	Will accommodate guests' special dietary needs

Egg Nog Cheesecake

Makes 10 to 12 Servings

"This is a wonderful holiday cheesecake." ~ Innkeeper, Austin Hill Inn

1¼	cups finely crushed vanilla wafers
3	tablespoons butter or margarine, melted
⅓	cup plus ½ cup sugar
1	envelope unflavored gelatin
1	cup canned or dairy eggnog
4	egg yolks, beaten
¼	teaspoon nutmeg
2	(8-ounce) packages cream cheese, softened
2	tablespoons rum
4	egg whites
½	cup whipping cream

Shaved chocolate or crushed vanilla wafers, for garnish (optional)

Preheat oven to 350°F. Combine vanilla wafers and butter; press into bottom and ½-inch up sides of a 9-inch springform pan to form a firm, even crust. Chill for 1 hour, or until firm.

Combine ⅓ cup sugar and gelatin in a saucepan. Stir in eggnog, egg yolks and nutmeg. Cook over medium heat, stirring constantly, until mixture just comes to a boil; remove from heat. In a large bowl, beat cream cheese with a mixer on medium speed for 30 seconds, or until softened. Gradually beat in gelatin mixture. Stir in rum. Chill until partially set.

In a medium bowl, beat egg whites with a mixer on medium speed until soft peaks form (tips fall). Gradually add ½ cup of sugar, beating to stiff peaks (tips stand straight). In a small bowl, beat cream to soft peaks. Fold egg whites and cream into gelatin mixture. Turn into pan. Cover and chill for several hours or overnight, until firm. Loosen sides of cheesecake from pan with a spatula. Remove sides. Sprinkle shaved chocolate or wafer crumbs around top edge of cheesecake to garnish.

Hartness House Inn

The Hartness House Inn is a historic country inn set on the beautiful 32-acre estate of a former governor of Vermont. Listed on the National Register of Historic Places, the inn offers landscaped grounds and gardens, an outdoor pool and park-like surroundings. A wide variety of accommodations are available, along with fine dining and casual restaurants, a tavern and an extensive wine cellar.

Near the inn, one can play tennis or golf, fly fish, antique shop, canoe, sail, hike, bike and enjoy glorious country drives with incomparable views.

INNKEEPERS:	Alla & Alex Leonenko
ADDRESS:	30 Orchard Street
	Springfield, Vermont 05156
TELEPHONE:	(802) 885-2115; (800) 732-4789
E-MAIL:	innkeeper@hartnesshouse.com
WEBSITE:	www.hartnesshouse.com
ROOMS:	42 Rooms; 2 Suites; Private baths
CHILDREN:	Welcome
ANIMALS:	Welcome; Call ahead; Resident cat
HANDICAPPED:	Handicapped accessible
DIETARY NEEDS:	Will accommodate guests' special dietary needs

Pumpkin Layer Cheesecake

Makes 8 to 12 Servings

2	(8-ounce) packages cream cheese, softened
½	cup sugar
½	teaspoon vanilla extract
2	large eggs
1	graham cracker crust
½	cup canned pumpkin
½	teaspoon cinnamon
¼	teaspoon ground cloves
¼	teaspoon nutmeg

Preheat oven to 350°F. Beat cream cheese, sugar and vanilla with a mixer on medium speed until well blended. Add eggs and beat well. Transfer 1 cup of cream cheese mixture to a small bowl; set aside and reserve. Spread remaining cream cheese mixture in crust.

Add pumpkin, cinnamon, cloves and nutmeg to reserved 1 cup of cream cheese mixture; mix well and carefully spread on top of cream cheese mixture in crust. Bake for 35-40 minutes. Cool cheesecake, then cover and chill for at least 3 hours before serving.

Three Bears at the Fountain

Three Bears at the Fountain Inn Bed & Breakfast is located just one mile north of Stowe's restaurants, shops, year-round activities and skiing at world-famous Stowe Resort. With a wraparound porch, perennial gardens and panoramic views of Mount Mansfield, the inn's setting invites relaxation and renewal.

The Fountain is one of Stowe's oldest homes. The actual fountain, for which the house is named, is fed by a mountain spring. In winter, it is a beautiful, towering ice sculpture that can be seen from the road and is a local landmark.

INNKEEPERS:	Suzanne & Stephen Vazzano
ADDRESS:	1049 Pucker Street Route 100
	Stowe, Vermont 05672
TELEPHONE:	(802) 253-7671; (800) 898-9634
E-MAIL:	threebears@stowevt.net
WEBSITE:	www.threebearsbandb.com
ROOMS:	4 Rooms; 2 Suites; Private baths
CHILDREN:	Children age 12 and older welcome
ANIMALS:	Not allowed; Resident small dog & cat
HANDICAPPED:	Not handicapped accessible
DIETARY NEEDS:	Will accommodate guests' special dietary needs

Pumpkin Whoopie Pies

Makes 15 to 20 Whoopie Pies

"Guests ask me for this recipe all the time." ~ Innkeeper, Three Bears at the Fountain Bed & Breakfast

Cookies:
- 1 cup sugar
- 1 stick butter, softened
- 2 large eggs
- 1 cup canned pumpkin
- 2 cups all-purpose flour
- 2 teaspoons baking powder
- 2 teaspoons cinnamon
- ½ teaspoon nutmeg
- ½ teaspoon ground ginger
- ¼ teaspoon ground cloves

Filling:
- ½ cup milk
- 3 tablespoons all-purpose flour
- 1 cup Crisco vegetable shortening
- ½ cup chopped pecans
- 1 cup powdered sugar
- ½ teaspoon vanilla extract
- 1 teaspoon maple extract
- ¼ teaspoon salt
- 1 cup marshmallow fluff

For the cookies: Preheat oven to 375°F. Beat sugar and butter. Beat in eggs and pumpkin. Stir in remaining ingredients. Drop dough by teaspoonsful onto a greased cookie sheet to make small circles. Bake for 9-10 minutes.

For the filling: Combine milk and flour in a saucepan over medium-low heat. Cook until thick; cool. In a bowl, beat milk mixture, Crisco, pecans, powdered sugar, vanilla and maple extract, salt and marshmallow fluff until light and fluffy. Make sandwiches with 2 cookies and filling.

Dockside Guest Quarters

For over 50 years, the Lusty family has welcomed guests to the Dockside Guest Quarters and Restaurant. Situated on a private, seven-acre peninsula bordering York Harbor and the ocean, the inn offers 21 rooms and suites. The Maine House is a classic New England cottage with a large wraparound porch. The view from the porch is quintessential coastal Maine, overlooking the harbor and the Atlantic ocean.

The Dockside Restaurant is set on the shores of Harris Island and is known for creatively prepared fresh Maine seafood in a yacht club atmosphere.

INNKEEPERS:	The Lusty Family
ADDRESS:	Harris Island Road
	York, Maine 03909
TELEPHONE:	(207) 363-2868; (800) 270-1977
E-MAIL:	info@docksidegq.com
WEBSITE:	www.docksideguestquarters.com
ROOMS:	15 Rooms; 6 Suites; Private baths
CHILDREN:	Children welcome
ANIMALS:	Not allowed
HANDICAPPED:	Handicapped accessible
DIETARY NEEDS:	Will accommodate guests' special dietary needs

Maine Maple Syrup Pie

Makes 8 Servings

"This is great on a cold day! A very rich and filling desert – delicious by itself or à la mode." ~ Innkeeper, Dockside Guest Quarters

1	cup maple syrup
1	pound brown sugar
1½	cups heavy cream
2	tablespoons butter, softened
4	eggs
1	(9-inch) pie crust

Vanilla ice cream, for serving

Preheat oven to 350°F. Beat together maple syrup, sugar, cream, butter and eggs. Pour into crust and bake for about 45 minutes, until a toothpick inserted in center comes out clean. Serve with ice cream, if desired.

Larchwood Inn

Located in the quaint, historic village of Wakefield in the town of South Kingstown, this beautiful country inn, surrounded by lawns and shaded by stately trees, has been dispensing gracious hospitality for over 160 years. The Larchwood Inn is just a short drive from Newport, the University of Rhode Island at Kingston, Mystic Seaport and much more.

Four dining rooms grace the Larchwood, serving delicious New England fare. After dinner, adjourn to the Tam O'Shanter Lounge for a cocktail, live entertainment, dancing and local humor.

INNKEEPERS:	Francis & Diann Browning
ADDRESS:	521 Main Street
	Wakefield Rhode Island 02879
TELEPHONE:	(401) 783-5454; (800) 275-5450
E-MAIL:	larchwoodinn@xpos.com
WEBSITE:	www.larchwoodinn.com
ROOMS:	18 Rooms; Private & shared baths
CHILDREN:	Children age 12 and older welcome
ANIMALS:	Not allowed
HANDICAPPED:	Not handicapped accessible
DIETARY NEEDS:	Will accommodate guests' special dietary needs

Larchwood Pie

Makes 2 Pies

½	cup cornstarch
1½	cups plus 6 tablespoons sugar
3	cups boiling water
6	egg whites
¾	teaspoon salt
2½	tablespoons vanilla extract
2½	tablespoons almond extract
2	pre-baked pie crusts

Whipped cream, for serving
Shaved bitter chocolate, for garnish

Preheat oven to 350°F. In a small bowl, combine cornstarch and 1½ cups of sugar; transfer to a medium saucepan. Add boiling water and cook over medium heat until mixture bubbles.

In a medium bowl, beat egg whites and salt with a mixer on high speed until stiff peaks form. While beating, gradually add 6 tablespoons of sugar and vanilla and almond extract. On medium speed, beat in cornstarch mixture. Divide filling among pie crusts and chill. Top with whipped cream and garnish with shaved chocolate to serve.

Adair Country Inn

Set on a grassy knoll on 200 acres of land near the White Mountains, this intimate inn has been hosting guests for nearly 75 years. Adair Country Inn, with its long drive bordered by stately pines, gleaming birch and stone walls, picturesque landscaping and graceful Colonial-revival design, is one of New England's most renowned inns.

"This luxury inn calls to the weary traveler from a snowy hilltop. Each room is exquisitely decorated with antiques and reproductions and has its own private bath. Personal touches abound." ~ *Connecticut Magazine*

INNKEEPERS:	Judy & Bill Whitman
ADDRESS:	80 Guider Lane
	Bethlehem, New Hampshire 03574
TELEPHONE:	(603) 444-2600; (888) 444-2600
E-MAIL:	innkeeper@adairinn.com
WEBSITE:	www.adairinn.com
ROOMS:	8 Rooms; 1 Suite; 1 Cottage; Private baths
CHILDREN:	Children age 12 and older welcome
ANIMALS:	Not allowed; Resident cat
HANDICAPPED:	Not handicapped accessible
DIETARY NEEDS:	Will accommodate guests' special dietary needs

Coconut Mousse with Clara Gold's Butterscotch Sauce

Makes 12 to 14 Servings

"This special recipe was the gift of a long-time friend and excellent cook, Debbie Flatley. It originated with her grandmother. I make it in brioche tins and serve the heavenly mixture on pretty dessert plates." ~ Innkeeper, Adair Country Inn

Coconut mousse:
- 3 tablespoons unflavored gelatin
- 3 cups milk, divided
- ⅔ cup sugar
- 2 teaspoons vanilla extract
- Pinch of salt
- 2 cups sweetened flaked coconut
- 2 cups heavy cream, whipped

Butterscotch sauce:
- 1¼ cups packed light brown sugar
- ⅔ cup light corn syrup
- ½ stick butter
- ½ cup whipping cream

For the mousse: Lightly oil a pan or mold, such as a Bundt or tube pan, individual molds or even a glass baking dish. Sprinkle gelatin over 1 cup of milk; let stand for 5 minutes to soften gelatin. Put remaining 2 cups of milk in a saucepan over low heat; add gelatin mixture and cook, stirring, until gelatin is dissolved. Stir in sugar, vanilla and salt. Chill until mixture thickens to the consistency of a thick sauce. Whisk to break up clumps. Fold in coconut and whipped cream. Pour mixture into pan or mold, cover tightly and refrigerate overnight or for up to 2 days. When ready to serve, prepare butterscotch sauce, then unmold mousse. Serve mousse with warm sauce.

For the sauce: In a heavy saucepan, bring sugar, corn syrup and butter to a boil. Boil until mixture reaches soft ball stage (a small amount of mixture dropped in a bowl of cold water forms a soft ball between your fingers), or a candy thermometer reads 240°F. Cool, then stir in cream until smooth.

Beach Plum Inn

On a cold November night in 1898, a raging storm swept over the island. From the wreckage of the schooners in Menemsha Harbor, wood was salvaged and a beautiful home was built. That house is now the Beach Plum Inn & Restaurant, a small inn overlooking the sea, where warm hospitality and outstanding cuisine combine in a naturally beautiful setting.

"The Beach Plum Inn should be on everyone's list. It is one of the most desirable country inns in America. This is the Vineyard … first class and unforgettable." ~ *Country Inns of New England*

INNKEEPERS:	The Arnold Family
ADDRESS:	50 Beach Plum Lane
	Menemsha, Massachusetts 02552
TELEPHONE:	(508) 645-9454; (877) 645-7398
E-MAIL:	info@beachpluminn.com
WEBSITE:	www.beachpluminn.com
ROOMS:	11 Rooms; Private baths
CHILDREN:	Children welcome
ANIMALS:	Not allowed
HANDICAPPED:	Handicapped accessible
DIETARY NEEDS:	Will accommodate guests' special dietary needs

Chocolate Chambord Soufflé

Makes 6 Servings

Soufflé base:
1	cup milk
2	teaspoons vanilla extract
⅓	cup plus 1 tablespoon all-purpose flour
⅓	cup plus 1 tablespoon sugar
4	egg yolks

Bring milk and vanilla just to a boil in a small saucepan, then remove from heat. Whisk together flour, sugar and eggs. Whisking constantly, slowly stream hot milk mixture into flour mixture. Return mixture to saucepan and cook over low heat for 5 minutes, stirring constantly. Strain and chill.

Soufflé:
Sugar for dusting ramekins plus ½ cup sugar
½	cup soufflé base
1	tablespoon Kahlúa
3	tablespoons Chambord or other raspberry liqueur
¼	cup melted semi-sweet chocolate (preferable Callebrout)
6	tablespoons raspberry purée, divided
8	egg yolks
6	egg whites

Powdered sugar, for garnish
Whipped cream, for serving

Preheat oven to 350°F. Brush 6 (6-ounce) ramekins with melted butter, then dust with sugar. In a stainless steel bowl, whisk together soufflé base, Kahlúa, Chambord, melted chocolate, 3 tablespoons of raspberry purée and egg yolks. Beat egg whites with a mixer on medium-high speed. As whites begin to thicken, add ½ cup of sugar and beat until soft peaks form. Gently fold egg whites into Kahlúa mixture; divide among ramekins. Immediately place ramekins in a baking pan filled half-full with hot water. Bake for about 20 minutes. Dust with powdered sugar. Serve immediately topped with whipped cream and drizzled with remaining 3 tablespoons of raspberry purée.

Geographic Listing of Bed & Breakfasts

Conneticut

Bristol	Chimney Crest Manor
Chester	Inn & Vineyard at Chester, The
Griswold	Homespun Farm
New Canaan	Roger Sherman Inn
Norfolk	Manor House
Old Saybrook	Deacon Timothy Pratt Bed & Breakfast Inn
Westbrook	Westbrook Inn

Massachusetts

Boston	Golden Slipper
Brewster	Brewster By the Sea
Chatham	Moses Nickerson House Inn
East Orleans	Parsonage Inn, The
Florence	Knoll, The
Freeport	Captain Briggs House Bed & Breakfast
Hyannis Port	Marston Family Bed & Breakfast
Lenox	Birchwood Inn
Lenox	Brook Farm Inn
Lenox	Gables Inn, The
Lenox	Gateways Inn
Marblehead	Harborside House
Marblehead	Seagull Inn Bed & Breakfast, The
Menemsha	Beach Plum Inn & Restaurant
Middleboro	1831 Zachariah Eddy House Bed & Breakfast
Nantucket	Sherburne Inn on Nantucket
Nantucket	Wauwinet, The
Rockport	Addison Choate Inn
Rockport	Inn on Cove Hill, The

Rockport	Yankee Clipper Inn
Somerville	Morrison House, The
Stockbridge	Arbor Rose Bed & Breakfast
Stockbridge	Inn at Stockbridge, The
West Barnstable	Honeysuckle Hill Bed & Breakfast
West Harwich	Cape Cod Claddagh Inn & Irish Pub
Yarmouth Port	One Center Street Inn

Maine

Bar Harbor	Primrose Inn
Bath	Pryor House
Belfast	Belfast Bay Meadows Inn
Blue Hill	Blue Hill Inn, The
Camden	Blue Harbor House, A Village Inn
Camden	Camden Windward House, The
Freeport	Harraseeket Inn
Kennebunkport	1802 House Inn
Kennebunkport	Maine Stay Inn & Cottages
Newcastle	Flying Cloud Bed & Breakfast, The
Ogunquit	Hartwell House Inn
Portland	Chadwick, The
Rockland	Captain Lindsey House Inn
Rockland	Lakeshore Inn
Searsport	1794 Watchtide by the Sea
Searsport	Inn Britannia
Southwest Harbor	Inn at Southwest, The
Spruce Head	Craignair Inn
Waterford	Bear Mountain Inn
Westbrook	Galen C. Moses House
York	Dockside Guest Quarters
York Harbor	York Harbor Inn

New Hampshire

Bethlehem	Adair Country Inn
Chocorua	Mt. Chocorua View House
Eaton Center	Inn at Crystal Lake
Henniker	Colby Hill Inn
Holderness	Inn on Golden Pond, The
Jackson	Crowes' Nest, The
Jaffrey	Benjamin Prescott Inn, The
Littleton	Beal House Inn & Restaurant
Loudon	Lovejoy Farm Bed & Breakfast
North Conway	1785 Inn & Restaurant, The
Portsmouth	Bow Street Inn, The
Rye	Arbor Inn Bed & Breakfast
Rye	Rock Ledge Manor
Sanbornton	Ferry Point House Bed & Breakfast
Shelburne	Mt. Washington Bed & Breakfast
Sugar Hill	Sugar Hill Inn

Rhode Island

Newport	1 Murray House Bed & Breakfast
Newport	1855 Marshall Slocum Guest House
Newport	Francis Malbone House, The
Newport	Wander Inn
Wakefield	Larchwood Inn
Westerly	Shelter Harbor Inn

Vermont

Arlington	Arlington's West Mountain Inn
Arlington	Hill Farm Inn
Jericho	Sinclair House Inn
Killington	Vermont Inn, The

Lower Waterford	Rabbit Hill Inn
Ludlow	Combs Family Inn, The
Ludlow	Echo Lake Inn
Lyndonville	Wild Flower Inn
Manchester Center	Inn at Ormsby Hill, The
Manchester Village	1811 House Bed & Breakfast
Newbury	Whipple Tree Bed & Breakfast, The
Pittsfield	Casa Bella Inn & Restaurant
Rutland	Inn at Rutland, The
Springfield	Hartness House Inn
Stowe	Brass Lantern Inn
Stowe	Siebeness - A Romantic Country Inn, The
Stowe	Stone Hill Inn
Stowe	Three Bears at the Fountain Bed & Breakfast
Vergennes	Strong House Inn
Wallingford	I. B. Munson House
Wallingford	White Rocks Inn Bed & Breakfast
Waterbury	Birds Nest Inn
Waterbury	Grunberg Haus
Waterbury	Inn at Blush Hill
West Dover	Austin Hill Inn
West Glover	Maple Manor Bed & Breakfast
Woodstock	Carriage House of Woodstock Bed & Breakfast
Woodstock	Deer Brook Inn
Woodstock	Silver Fox Farm
Woodstock	Winslow House, The

Alphabetical Listing of Bed & Breakfasts

1 Murray House Bed & Breakfast 154

1785 Inn & Restaurant, The 216, 252

1794 Watchtide by the Sea 52, 138

1802 House Inn...118

1811 House Bed & Breakfast 268, 282

1831 Zachariah Eddy House Bed & Breakfast..............................144, 238

1855 Marshall Slocum Guest House 198

Adair Country Inn..86, 300

Addison Choate Inn 142

Arbor Inn Bed & Breakfast 60, 130

Arbor Rose Bed & Breakfast 44

Arlington's West Mountain Inn 180

Austin Hill Inn 290

Beach Plum Inn & Restaurant...200, 302

Beal House Inn & Restaurant 208, 256

Bear Mountain Inn 82

Belfast Bay Meadows Inn..116

Benjamin Prescott Inn, The 42

Birchwood Inn..98, 162

Birds Nest Inn 88, 270

Blue Harbor House, A Village Inn..204

Blue Hill Inn, The 174, 218

Bow Street Inn, The..8

Brass Lantern Inn 120

Brewster By the Sea 258, 266

Brook Farm Inn..110

Camden Windward House, The	90
Cape Cod Claddagh Inn & Irish Pub	248
Captain Briggs House Bed & Breakfast	152
Captain Lindsey House Inn	48
Carriage House of Woodstock Bed & Breakfast	32
Casa Bella Inn & Restaurant	226
Chadwick, The	146
Chimney Crest Manor	84
Colby Hill Inn	36, 150
Combes Family Inn, The	254
Craignair Inn	92
Crowes' Nest, The	236
Deacon Timothy Pratt Bed & Breakfast Inn	34
Deer Brook Inn	230
Dockside Guest Quarters	296
Echo Lake Inn	182, 214
Ferry Point House Bed & Breakfast	124
Flying Cloud Bed & Breakfast, The	172, 210
Francis Malbone House, The	278, 286
Gables Inn, The	12
Galen C. Moses House	132
Gateways Inn	206, 272
Golden Slipper	288
Grunberg Haus	156
Harborside House	276
Harraseeket Inn	190, 222
Hartness House Inn	292
Hartwell House Inn	26, 56

Hill Farm Inn	64, 194
Homespun Farm	18
Honeysuckle Hill Bed & Breakfast	168, 246
I. B. Munson House	106
Inn & Vineyard at Chester, The	112
Inn at Blush Hill	80
Inn at Crystal Lake	10, 264
Inn at Ormsby Hill, The	114
Inn at Rutland, The	108
Inn at Southwest, The	16
Inn at Stockbridge, The	44, 186
Inn Britannia	134
Inn on Cove Hill, The	30
Inn on Golden Pond, The	38
Knoll, The	40
Lakeshore Inn	50
Larchwood Inn	298
Lovejoy Farm Bed & Breakfast	166
Maine Stay Inn & Cottages	58, 78
Manor House	94
Maple Manor Bed & Breakfast	66
Marston Family Bed & Breakfast	250
Morrison House, The	14
Moses Nickerson House Inn	158
Mt. Chocorua View House	170
Mt. Washington Bed & Breakfast	102
One Center Street Inn	100
Parsonage Inn, The	136

Primrose Inn	202, 284
Pryor House	122, 148
Rabbit Hill Inn	20, 178
Rock Ledge Manor	76
Roger Sherman Inn	176
Seagull Inn Bed & Breakfast, The	62
Shelter Harbor Inn	164
Sherburne Inn on Nantucket	260
Siebeness - A Romantic Country Inn, The	70
Silver Fox Farm	74
Sinclair House Inn	240
Stone Hill Inn	224
Strong House Inn	184
Sugar Hill Inn	28, 72
Three Bears at the Fountain Bed & Breakfast	294
Vermont Inn, The	228
Wander Inn	242
Wauwinet, The	188, 220
Westbrook Inn	24
Whipple-Tree Bed & Breakfast, The	54
White Rocks Inn Bed & Breakfast	22, 244
Wild Flower Inn	104
Winslow House, The	140, 274
Yankee Clipper Inn	280
York Harbor Inn	196, 232

Index

A

ALMONDS
- Banana Oatmeal Almond Muffins, 31
- Chocolate Raspberry Almond Delights, 275
- Primrose Coconut "Joys", 285

APPLES (and APPLESAUCE)
- Apple or Carrot Bran Muffins, 45
- Apple Clafouti, 87
- Apple Crêpes, 121
- Apple Ginger Upside-Down French Toast, 99
- Apple Muffins, 41
- Apple Raisin Bread Pudding, 119
- Apple Waffles with Apple Cider Syrup, 93
- Apple Walnut Cream Scones, 61
- Applesauce Currant Cake, 55
- Carmel Apple Pumpkin Pancakes, 71
- Caramelized Apple Bread Pudding, 113
- Catherine's Tarte Tatin, 257
- Cranberry Apple Coffee Cake, 51
- Curried Vermont Apple Soup, 183
- Flying Cloud Breakfast Sausage Patties, 173
- Maple-Apple Waffles with Ben & Jerry's Ice Cream, 89
- Maine Apple Cake, 53
- Nantucket Cranberry Apple Crisp, 261
- Oatmeal Apple Pancakes, 79
- Turkey, Apple & Pecan Salad, 191

APPETIZERS (see Index on Page 192)

ARTICHOKES
- Elegant Artichoke Dip, 197
- Smoked Salmon & Artichoke Frittata, 141
- Wauwinet Lobster "Cobb" Salad, 189

ASPARAGUS
- Goat Cheese, Asparagus & Spring Onion Frittata, 143

B

BANANAS
- Banana Bread French Toast, 101
- Banana Bread with Streusel Topping, 15
- Banana Oatmeal Almond Muffins, 31
- Drunken Bananas, 241
- French Banana Crêpes, 123
- Strawberry Banana French Toast, 107

BEEF
- Autumn Brisket, 231

BLUEBERRIES
- Blueberry Cream Muffins, 43
- Blueberry Gingerbread, 17
- Blueberry Morning Glory, 111
- Blueberry Sage Scones, 57
- Blueberry Sour Cream Cake, 49
- Bobby's Blueberry Bread, 11
- Four-Berry Pancakes, 81
- Fresh Blueberry Pie, 253
- Lemon Blueberry Pancakes, 77
- Sour Cream, Peach & Blueberry Pancakes, 83
- Strawberry Peach Compote in Sweet Wine Syrup, 239
- Wicked Good Belgian Waffles with Maine Blueberry Compote, 91

BREADS (see Index on Page 6)
BREAD PUDDINGS (see Index on Page 96)

C

CAKES (see Index on Page 262)
CHEESE
- Boursin:

Lobster Stuffed Chicken with Boursin Cheese Sauce, 233
Three Late Afternoon Dips, 199
Brie:
　Crabby Brie Souffles, 129
Cheddar:
　Ham & Potato Pie, 155
　Herb-Baked Eggs, 137
　Lobster Breakfast Treat, 153
　Nantucket Pie, 159
　Potato Pancakes with Poached Eggs & Cheddar, 151
　Potluck Potatoes, 169
　Pryor House Sausage Quiche, 149
　Vermont Baked Veal, 229
　Vermont Cheddar Pie, 157
　Vermont Cheddar Wafers, 27
Cream Cheese:
　Blueberry Morning Glory, 111
　Blackberry- Stuffed French Toast, 105
　Egg Nog Cheesecake, 291
　Elegant Artichoke Dip, 197
　Fresh Blueberry Pie, 253
　Garlic Chive Potato Pancakes, 171
　Pumpkin Layer Cheesecake, 293
　Salmon Pâté, 195
　Three Late Afternoon Dips, 199
Feta:
　Vermont Cheddar Pie, 157
Goat:
　Caramelized Onion & Goat Cheese Tart, 207
　Goat Cheese, Asparagus & Spring Onion Frittata, 143
　Goat Cheese Popovers, 23
Gouda:
　Egg Blossoms, 131
Gruyère:
　Smoked Salmon Ravioli, 217
Jarlsberg:
　Savory Smoked Atlantic Salmon Clafoutti, 139
Mascarpone:
　Gingerbread Mascarpone Petite Fours, 273
　Pears in Mascarpone Custard, 237
Monterey Jack:
　Lobster Quiche, 145
Mozzarella:
　Nantucket Pie, 159
　Portobello Venezia, 209
　Westbrook Inn Spinach Bread, 25
Parmesan:
　Cornish Baked Eggs, 135
　Lobster Quiche, 145
　Potluck Potatoes, 169
Provolone:
　Westbrook Inn Spinach Bread, 25
Ricotta:
　Stuffed Portobello Mushrooms with Sun-Dried Tomato Purée, 211
Romano:
　Vermont Cheddar Pie, 157
　Westbrook Inn Spinach Bread, 25
Swiss:
　Crab Quiche, 147
　Pryor House Sausage Quiche, 149

CHICKEN
　Lobster Stuffed Chicken with Boursin Cheese Sauce, 233

CHOCOLATE
　1811 House Brownies, 283
　Cappuccino Chocolate Chip Muffins, 35
　Chocolate Chambord Souffle, 303
　Chocolate Walnut Bars, 279
　Chocolate Raspberry Almond Delights, 275
　Chocolate Walnut Espresso Biscotti, 277

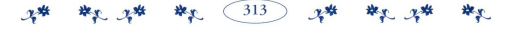

Coconut Chocolate Chip Cookies, 267
Crunchy Chocolate Chip Cookies, 269
Double Chocolate Chip Cookies, 265
Gingerbread Mascarpone Petite Fours, 273
"Oh Henry" Bars, 281
Primrose Coconut "Joys", 285
Pumpkin Chocolate Chip Muffins, 33

COCONUT
   Apple or Carrot Bran Muffins, 45
   Coconut Chocolate Chip Cookies, 267
   Coconut Mousse with Clara Gold's Butterscotch Sauce, 301
   Hill Farm Granola, 65
   Primrose Coconut "Joys", 285

COFFEE CAKES (see Index on Page 46)
COOKIES (see Index on Page 262)
CORN (and CORNMEAL)
   Blue Harbor House Crab Cakes, 205
   Blue & Yellow Cornmeal Layered Pound Cake, 21
   Corn & Wild Rice Cakes with Smoked Salmon, 201
   Indian Summer Corn Cakes, 163
   Lobster Saute, 223

CRAB
   Blue Harbor House Crab Cakes, 205
   Crab Quiche, 147
   Crab & Shrimp Egg Toasts, 203
   Crabby Brie Souffles, 129

CRANBERRIES & DRIED CRANBERRIES
   Chocolate Walnut Espresso Biscotti, 277
   Claddagh Cranberry Conserve & Chutney, 249
   Cranberry Apple Coffee Cake, 51
   Cranberry Bread Pudding, 115
   Cranberry-Orange Christmas Bread, 13
   Cranberry & Pecan-Filled Squash, 175
   Cranberry Scones, 63
   Double Chocolate Chip Cookies, 265
   Hill Farm Granola, 65
   Maine Apple Cake, 53
   Nantucket Cranberry Apple Crisp, 261

CREPES (see Index on Page 96)

D
DESSERTS (see Index on Page 262)

E
EGG DISHES (see Index on Page 126)

F
FRENCH TOAST (see Index on Page 96)

L
LOBSTER
   Lobster Breakfast Treat, 153
   Lobster Gazpacho, 179
   Lobster Quiche, 145
   Lobster Saute, 223
   Lobster Stuffed Chicken with Boursin Cheese Sauce, 233
   New England Lobster Bisque, 177
   Wauwinet Lobster "Cobb" Salad, 189

M
MANGO
   Mango Smoothie, 251

MAPLE SYRUP
   Baked Eggs in Maple Toast Cups, 133
   Banana Bread French Toast, 101
   Blueberry Morning Glory, 111
   Flying Cloud Breakfast Sausage Patties, 173
   Maine Apple Cake, 53
   Maine Maple Syrup Pie, 297
   Maple-Apple Waffles, 89
   Maple Butter Cookies, 271
   Maple Oatmeal Scones, 59
   Maple Pumpkin Bisque, 181
   Maple Walnut Muffins, 29

Pumpkin Yogurt, 167
Wicked Good Belgian Waffles with
   Maine Blueberry Compote, 91
MUFFINS (see Index on Page 6)
MUSHROOMS
   Blue Harbor House Crab Cakes, 205
   Portobello Venezia, 209
   Stuffed Portobello Mushrooms with
     Sun-Dried Tomato Purée, 211
   Westbrook Inn Spinach Bread, 25

N
NUTS (see Almonds, Pecans & Walnuts)

O
OATS/OATMEAL
   Apple Muffins, 41
   Banana Oatmeal Almond Muffins, 31
   Crunchy Chocolate Chip Cookies. 269
   Double Chocolate Chip Cookies, 265
   Hill Farm Granola, 65
   Irish Oatmeal, 67
   Maple Oatmeal Scones, 59
   Maple Walnut Muffins, 29
   Nantucket Cranberry Apple Crisp, 261
   Oatmeal Apple Pancakes, 79
   "Oh Henry" Bars, 281
   Sour Cream Rhubarb Streusel Pie, 255
ORANGES
   Apple Crêpes, 121
   Banana Bread French Toast, 101
   Caramelized Nantucket Bay Scallops with
     Upland Cress, Cucumbers & Sesame
     Vinaigrette, 221
   Chocolate Raspberry Almond Delights,
     275
   Cranberry-Orange Christmas Bread, 13
   Cranberry Scones, 63

Flat-Top Orange Date Muffins, 39
Orange Waffles, 95
Raisin Pecan French Toast, 109
Strawberries Romanoff, 243
Wauwinet Lobster "Cobb" Salad, 189

P
PANCAKES (see Index on Page 68)
PEACHES
   Baked Peaches with Raspberries & Cream,
     245
   Catherine's Tarte Tatin, 257
   Sour Cream, Peach & Blueberry Pancakes, 83
   Strawberry Peach Compote in Sweet Wine
     Syrup, 239
PEARS
   Pears in Mascarpone Custard, 237
PECANS
   Cranberry & Pecan-Filled Squash, 175
   Pull-Apart Bread, 19
   Pumpkin Whoopie Pies, 295
   Raisin Pecan French Toast, 109
   Salmon Pâté, 195
   Three Late Afternoon Dips, 199
   Turkey, Apple & Pecan Salad, 191
PEPPERS
   Elegant Artichoke Dip, 197
   Ham & Potato Pie, 155
   Lobster Gazpacho, 179
   Roasted Red Pepper Soup, 185
   Westbrook Inn Spinach Bread, 25
PIES
   Larchwood Pie, 299
   Maine Maple Syrup Pie, 297
   Pumpkin Whoopie Pies, 295
   Sour Cream Rhubarb Streusel Pie, 255
PLUMS
   Bohemian Plum Dumplings, 247

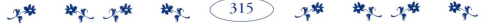

Plum Torte, 259
PORK
  Bacon:
    Egg Blossoms, 131
    Nantucket Pie, 159
    Vermont Baked Veal, 229
  Ham:
    Ham & Potato Pie, 155
    Herb-Baked Eggs, 137
  Pancetta:
    Wauwinet Lobster "Cobb" Salad, 189
  Prosciutto:
    Portobello Venezia, 209
  Sausage:
    Flying Cloud Breakfast Sausage Patties, 173
    Pryor House Sausage Quiche, 149
POTATOES (and SWEET POTATOES)
  Bohemian Plum Dumplings, 247
  Easy Potato Leek Soup, 187
  Garlic Chive Potato Pancakes, 171
  Ham & Potato Pie, 155
  Lobster Saute, 223
  Nantucket Pie, 159
  New England Lobster Bisque, 177
  Portobello Venezia, 209
  Potato Pancakes with Poached Eggs & Cheddar, 151
  Potluck Potatoes, 169
  Roasted Red Pepper Soup, 185
  Sweet Potato Muffins or Bread, 37
  Vermont Cheddar Pie, 157
PUMPKIN
  Carmel Apple Pumpkin Pancakes, 71
  Maple Pumpkin Bisque, 181
  Pumpkin Bread Pudding, 117
  Pumpkin Chocolate Chip Muffins, 33
  Pumpkin Layer Cheesecake, 293
  Pumpkin Whoopie Pie, 295
  Pumpkin Yogurt, 167

Q
QUICHES (see Index on Page 126)

R
RASPBERRIES
  Baked Peaches with Raspberries & Cream, 245
  Chocolate Chambord Souffle, 303
  Chocolate Raspberry Almond Delights, 275
  Four-Berry Pancakes, 81

S
SALADS (see Index on Page 160)
SALMON
  Corn & Wild Rice Cakes with Smoked Salmon, 201
  Salmon Pâté, 195
  Savory Smoked Atlantic Salmon Clafoutti, 139
  Scallop-Stuffed Salmon en Papillote, 215
  Smoked Salmon & Artichoke Frittata, 141
  Smoked Salmon Ravioli, 217

SCALLOPS
  Caramelized Nantucket Bay Scallops with Cucumbers, Upland Cress & Sesame Vinaigrette, 221
  Pan-Seared Scallops with Capers & Lemon, 219
  Scallop-Stuffed Salmon en Papillote, 215
SCONES (see Index on Page 46)
SEAFOOD (see Crab, Lobster, Scallops, Shrimp & Squid)
SHRIMP
  Crab & Shrimp Egg Toasts. 203
  Mediterranean Shrimp, 225

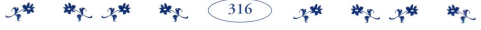

SIDE DISHES (see Index on Page 160)
SOUPS (see Index on Page 160)
SPINACH
  Egg Blossoms, 131
  Lobster Breakfast Treat, 153
  Vermont Baked Veal, 229
  Vermont Cheddar Pie, 157
  Westbrook Inn Spinach Bread, 25
SQUID
  Calamari Alla Franco, 227
STRAWBERRIES
  Four-Berry Pancakes, 81
  Strawberry Banana French Toast, 107
  Strawberry Peach Compote in Sweet
    Wine Syrup, 239
  Strawberries Romanoff, 243

T
TOMATOES
  Savory Smoked Atlantic Salmon Clafoutti, 139
  New England Lobster Bisque, 177
  Lobster Gazpacho, 179
  Roasted Red Pepper Soup, 185
  Stuffed Portobello Mushrooms with Sun-Dried Tomato Purée, 211
  Calamari Alla Franco, 227
TURKEY
  Turkey, Apple & Pecan Salad, 191

V
VEAL
  Vermont Baked Veal, 229

W
WAFFLES (see Index on Page 68)
WALNUTS
  1811 House Brownies, 283
  Apple Muffins, 41
  Apple Walnut Cream Scones, 61
  Banana Bread with Streusel Topping, 15
  Chocolate Walnut Bars, 279
  Chocolate Walnut Espresso Biscotti, 277
  Claddagh Cranberry Conserve & Chutney, 249
  Coconut Chocolate Chip Cookies, 267
  Double Chocolate Chip Cookies, 265
  Maine Apple Cake, 53
  Maple Butter Cookies, 271
  Maple Walnut Muffins, 29
  Sweet Potato Muffins or Bread, 37

Z
ZUCCHINI category
  Goat Cheese, Asparagus & Spring Onion Frittata, 143
  Lobster Gazpacho, 179

The Bed & Breakfast Cookbook Series

Entertain with ease and flair! B&B's and Country Inns from across the nation share their best and most requested recipes. More than just a recipe collection, each book in the Bed & Breakfast Cookbook Series will help you choose the perfect B&B for your next getaway.

California Bed & Breakfast Cookbook
From the Warmth & Hospitality of 127 B&B's and Country Inns throughout California. Book #5 in the series.
$19.95 / 328pp / ISBN 1-889593-11-7

Colorado Bed & Breakfast Cookbook
From the Warmth & Hospitality of 88 Colorado B&B's and Country Inns. Book #1 in the series! New 2nd Edition.
$19.95 / 320pp / ISBN 0-9653751-0-2

New England Bed & Breakfast Cookbook
From the Warmth & Hospitality of 107 B&B's and Country Inns in CT, MA, ME, NH, RI & VT. Book #6 in the series.
$19.95 / 320pp / ISBN 1-889593-12-5

Texas Bed & Breakfast Cookbook
From the Warmth & Hospitality of 70 B&B's, Guest Ranches and Country Inns throughout the Lone Star State. Book #3 in the series.
$19.95 / 320pp / ISBN 1-889593-07-9

Virginia Bed & Breakfast Cookbook
From the Warmth & Hospitality of 76 Virginia B&B's and Country Inns. Book #4 in the series.
$19.95 / 320pp / ISBN 1-889593-09-5

Washington State Bed & Breakfast Cookbook
From the Warmth & Hospitality of 72 Washington State B&B's and Country Inns. Book #2 in the series. New 2nd Edition.
$19.95 / 320pp / ISBN 1-889593-05-2

❋ Coming Soon: *North Carolina Bed & Breakfast Cookbook* (Fall, 2004) and *Georgia Bed & Breakfast Cookbook* and *New York Bed & Breakfast Cookbook* (Spring, 2005). ❋

Bed & Breakfast Cookbook Series Order Form

655 BROADWAY, SUITE 560, DENVER, CO 80203
888-456-3607 • www.3dpress.net • orders@3dpress.net

PLEASE SEND ME:

	Price	Quantity
CALIFORNIA BED & BREAKFAST COOKBOOK	$19.95	_____
COLORADO BED & BREAKFAST COOKBOOK	$19.95	_____
NEW ENGLAND BED & BREAKFAST COOKBOOK	$19.95	_____
NORTH CAROLINA BED & BREAKFAST COOKBOOK	$19.95	_____
TEXAS BED & BREAKFAST COOKBOOK	$19.95	_____
VIRGINIA BED & BREAKFAST COOKBOOK	$19.95	_____
WASHINGTON STATE BED & BREAKFAST COOKBOOK	$19.95	_____

SUBTOTAL: $ _____

Colorado residents add 3.8% sales tax. Denver residents add 7.2% $ _____

Add $5.00 for shipping for 1st book, add $1 for each additional $ _____

TOTAL ENCLOSED: $ _____

*Special offer: Buy any 2 books in the series and take a 10% discount. Buy 4 or more books and take a 25% discount!

SEND TO:

Name _____

Address _____

City _____ State _____ Zip _____

Phone _____ A gift from: _____

We accept checks, money orders, Visa or Mastercard. Please make checks payable to 3D Press, Inc.

Please charge my ☐ VISA ☐ MASTERCARD

Card Number _____ Expiration Date _____